THE PRESBYTERIAN CHURCH IN IRELAND

Finlay Holmes

The Presbyterian Church in Ireland
A Popular History

the columba press

First published in 2000 by
the columba press
55A Spruce Avenue, Stillorgan Industrial Park,
Blackrock, Co Dublin

Cover by Bill Bolger
Origination by The Columba Press
Printed in Ireland by Colour Books Ltd, Dublin

ISBN 1 85607 284 3

Contents

Introduction

I was glad to have the invitation of The Columba Press to write a popular history of Irish Presbyterianism. It gave me an opportunity to revise and simplify my earlier history, *Our Irish Presbyterian Heritage*, published in 1985 for the Publications Board of the Irish Presbyterian Church and intended primarily for Presbyterian church members. It is hoped that this popular history will inform a wider public about Irish Presbyterianism, who they are, where they have come from and what they have done and are doing in their obedience to Christ.

Frequently caricatured as dour bigots, that is not how they see themselves, and if we are to understand the Irish historical experience since the early seventeenth century, we need to take into account their distinctive role in that experience. Why was it, for example, that some Presbyterians were prominent among the founding fathers of Irish Republicanism in the late eighteenth century and participated in the 1798 rebellion against British rule in Ireland, yet most Irish Presbyterians became ardent Unionists in the course of the nineteenth century?

Quotations in the text indicate my indebtedness to many other historians and I have provided a select bibliography to acknowledge that indebtedness more specifically.

Finally, my thanks are due to Seán O Boyle and The Columba Press for their helpfulness in the process of publication and to my wife, Josephine, great grand-daughter of the first Irish Presbyterian missionary to China, who has encouraged me to complete this history and have more time to enjoy the leisure of retirement and see more of our seven grandchildren.

Finlay Holmes

CHAPTER 1

The First Presbyterians in Ireland

Irish Presbyterianism cannot be said to be an indigenous Irish phenomenon though many Irish Presbyterians feel a strong kinship with St Patrick and early Irish Christianity. Presbyterianism came to Ireland with Scottish immigrants in the seventeenth century. A glance at the map shows how close together the south west of Scotland and the north east of Ireland are. For centuries people and ideas have been crossing the narrow stretch of water between the two countries. This was probably the route taken by Ireland's first inhabitants 7000 years before Christ. A movement of population eastward from Ireland in the fifth century gave Scotland its name as the land of the *Scotti,* Latin for Irish, and the Irish Christian community founded by Columba in 563 contributed significantly to the evangelisation of 'Scotland' and north Britain. A thousand years later, a movement of population westward from Scotland to Ireland brought Presbyterianism to Ireland

Presbyterianism had taken root in Scotland in the course of the sixteenth-century movement of reformation in the church in Western Europe. *The Dogmatic Constitution of the Church* of the Second Vatican Council declares that 'The church ... is always in need of being purified and incessantly pursues the path of penance and renewal.' The path of renewal in the sixteenth century brought new life to the church but also division. The old bottles of traditional church order, doctrine and discipline were not always able to contain the new wine of reformation, and Presbyterianism was one of the new bottles to take shape, involving a radical re-ordering of the church's structures and life in obedience to what reformers like the Frenchman, Jean Cauvin

(Latin, *Calvinus,* English, *Calvin*) in Geneva believed to be the teaching of Scripture. The teaching of Scripture, rather than church tradition, was to be authoritative in all questions of belief and practice. At the centre of Presbyterianism, its theology and worship, is Scripture, the word of God.

The words *Presbyterian* and *Presbyterianism* describe the form of government and organisation of what became known as the Reformed Church, emphasising continuity with the One, Holy, Catholic and Apostolic Church, for reformers like Calvin did not believe that they were founding new churches. They were re-forming the church, bringing her back to her New Testament origins. The New Testament church, they contended, had been Presbyterian, rather than Episcopalian, in government.

Both these words, *presbyterian* and *episcopalian,* come from words in the Greek New Testament – *presbuteros,* a presbyter or elder, and *episkopos,* a bishop. Calvin argued that, in the New Testament, bishops were presbyters and presbyters bishops, that they were interchangeable terms, as in Acts chapter 20, where Paul appears to call the church leaders in Ephesus both presbyters and bishops. The Presbyterian form of church government, as developed by Calvin's disciples, Theodore Beza in Geneva, John Knox in Scotland and Thomas Cartwright in England, offered an alternative to the episcopal system of oversight and leadership which had characterised the Pre-Reformation church and which, in their view, had failed the church. They could not see in delinquent pluralists like Albrecht of Brandenburg, whose shabby arrangements with the papacy to raise money to defray the cost of his pluralism and simony by selling indulgences provoked Martin Luther's protest in 1517, as the successors of the apostles.

These reformers believed that, in the apostolic church, oversight was provided, not by individual apostles or bishops but by councils of presbyter/bishops, a *presbuterion*. Therefore they replaced the hierarchical episcopal structure of church government by a series of councils or consistories under a synod or general assembly as the supreme governing body of a territorial or national church. A revolutionary feature of these councils or consistories was the participation of elders, who were not ministers of word and sacrament, but essentially laymen, although, later, they underwent a form of ordination.

Kings and princes who had been accustomed to exercise some control over the church by judicious episcopal appointments disliked Presbyterianism, which made control of the church more difficult. Presbyterians, on the other hand, were conscientiously opposed to any form of Erastianism – the control of the church by the state – claiming that Jesus Christ himself was the sole king and head of the church and his kingship and headship could not be compromised. Christ is Lord, to quote an early Christian credal affirmation, and his authority could not be shared with any other authority, civil or ecclesiastical.

James VI of Scotland, later to be James I of the United Kingdom, believing that he was king by divine right, God's lieutenant on earth, disliked being told by Presbyterians like Andrew Melville that, in the church, he was not a king, but merely a member, the subject of Jesus, the king and head of the church. Predictably James came to the view that monarchy and Presbyterianism were incompatible and he determined that Presbyterianism must either be extirpated or in some way subjected to the royal will. It was of course the fact that, unlike the Reformation in England, the Scottish Reformation had been led, not by the Crown, but by preachers like John Knox and nobles calling themselves the 'Lords of the Congregation of Jesus Christ', who doubtless had their own agenda, which had contributed to the success of Presbyterianism in Scotland.

James embarked upon a subtle campaign to weaken the power of the Scottish General Assembly and restore episcopacy in Scotland. In neighbouring England, Elizabeth had defeated the attempts of Presbyterians like Thomas Cartwright, professor of divinity at Cambridge, to make the Church of England a Presbyterian Church, and when James succeeded her in 1603, he quickly made it clear that, although he was a Scot, he was not going to advance the Presbyterian cause. In fact he used his new authority to intensify his campaign against Presbyterianism in Scotland, succeeding in restoring episcopacy in 1610 and such Catholic practices as kneeling for communion and observing saints' days, both abhorrent to Presbyterians as unscriptural and 'popish'. Some of the Scots Presbyterian ministers who came to Ireland in the early seventeenth century did so in the hope of finding greater freedom in Ireland to follow the Presbyterian way.

Such success as the Protestant Reformation had enjoyed in Scotland and England had not been paralleled in Ireland. By the end of the sixteenth century, the reformed Church of Ireland, the church by law established, had certainly not become the church of a majority of the Irish people. One area in which it was virtually non-existent was in the northern province of Ulster, one of the last strongholds of Gaelic Irish independence. The situation there had changed, however, when James succeeded Elizabeth, with the defeat of Ulster's Gaelic chieftains after a bitter nine years' struggle. Although the defeated chieftains, the O'Neill, Earl of Tyrone, the O'Donnell, Earl of Tyrconnell, and their followers, were treated generously and allowed to continue in their patrimonies, their independent power was greatly diminished and they faced an uncertain future with the prospect of increasing Dublin government control and advancing anglicisation.

Their discomfort and anxieties led to the so-called Flight of the Earls in 1607, when the flower of Ulster's Gaelic aristocracy, led by O'Neill and O'Donnell, sailed from Rathmullan in Donegal to seek security in Catholic Europe with the hope of finding support to recover their heritage. The government responded by confiscating their lands, thus opening the way for the massive enterprise of colonisation known as the Plantation of Ulster.

The union of the kingdoms of Scotland, England, Wales and Ireland in 1603 had opened up the prospect of Scottish emigration to nearby Ulster. Hitherto Scottish immigrants had not been welcome in Ireland, although the MacDonnells, Lords of the Isles, had established themselves in north-east Antrim as early as 1399, when John Mor MacDonnell had married Margery

Bisset, heiress of lands acquired by Norman invaders in the twelfth century. Although Sir Randal MacDonnell was a Catholic who had supported the Gaelic chieftains in the Nine Years' War, he enjoyed James I's favour and was encouraged to bring Scottish tenants into Ulster, some of whom were lowland Scots and Protestants. Other Scots were turning acquisitive eyes towards Ireland. James allowed two Ayrshire men, James Hamilton, son of the minister of Dunlap, and Hugh Montgomery, Laird of Braidstone, to share in the dismemberment of the county Down lands of the impoverished Conn O'Neill, who was languishing in prison. O'Neill's part in the bargain was release from prison and a pardon for his alleged offences. The interest of the Crown was that 'the sea coasts might be possessed by Scottish men who would be traders as proper to his majesty's future advantage'. This was the beginning of the colonisation of Antrim and Down by lowland Scots which prepared the way for the later and more extensive colonisation of Armagh, Coleraine (later Londonderry), Cavan, Fermanagh, Tyrone and Donegal – the Plantation of Ulster.

The settlements in Antrim and Down had not exhausted the number of potential colonists from Scotland. According to Sir William Alexander, founder of the unsuccessful Scottish colony of Nova Scotia in 1620 and who acquired land in Armagh and Donegal, Scotland 'by reason of her populousnesse, being constrained to disburthen herself like the painful bees did every yeere send forth swarmes'. There had been unsuccessful attempts by lowland Scots to colonise the island of Lewis, but now Ulster, with cheap land available on attractive terms, under the protection of the English Crown, offered new possibilities for the upwardly mobile and those needing to repair declining fortunes or make a fresh start in life.

The colonists did not come, originally, as any kind of ecclesiastical missionaries. Certainly some of the ministers who followed them from Scotland did not regard them as exemplary members of the Reformed Church. One of those ministers, Robert Blair of Bangor, judged that:

although amongst those men divine providence did send to
Ireland there were several persons eminent for birth, education and parts, yet for the most part were such as either
poverty, scandalous lives or, at the best adventurers seeking
better accommodation.

Neither Reformation nor Counter-Reformation had made
much progress in Ulster. The damning verdict of Sir John Davies,
the Irish Attorney-General, on the state of religion in Ireland
was particularly true of Ulster:

> The churches are ruined and fallen down ... There is no di-
> vine service, no christening of children, no receiving of the
> sacrament, no Christian meetings or assembly, no, not once a
> year; in a word no more demonstration of religion than
> amongst Tartars or cannibals.

Emissaries of both Reformation and Counter-Reformation
who came to Ireland were at one in their opinion that the Irish
were essentially pagan. Davies believed that an active preaching
ministry, particularly if offered in the Gaelic language of the
Irish people, could transform the situation. However, the Church
of Ireland was short of active, preaching ministers and shorter
still of those who could preach in Gaelic. The first Church of
Ireland Bishop of Derry, Raphoe and Clogher – later to be separate bishoprics – was a Gaelic speaking Scot, Denis Campbell,
who had been Dean of Limerick, but he died before he could assume his episcopal responsibilities and his successor, another
Scot, George Montgomery, brother of Hugh Montgomery, the
county Down colonist, had no Gaelic, having formerly been
Dean of Norwich.

It was significant for future ecclesiastical developments in
Ulster that these first bishops and their successors were Scots
who had had experience of Presbyterianism in Scotland.
Andrew Knox, who succeeded Montgomery in Raphoe in 1610,
had been ordained by the Presbytery of Paisley in 1581. Men like
Knox were familiar with the Scottish situation in which, even
after the restoration of episcopacy in 1610, elements of Presbyterianism survived. Bishops sometimes acted as bishops in

presbytery, presbyters acting with them in ordinations. Undoubtedly this facilitated the ordination and installation in Church of Ireland parishes in Ulster of Scottish ministers who were Presbyterians. They were welcome because of the shortage of clergy and because, as Dean Leslie, later Bishop of Down, and another Scot, observed, 'in many places a minister as good as none, a dumb dog that cannot bark'.

Certainly some of the Scottish ministers who came to Ulster were not dumb dogs who could not bark. Men like Robert Blair of Bangor or John Livingstone of Killinchy were among the most gifted ministers in the contemporary Scottish church. Blair had taught philosophy in Glasgow University but was unhappy about developments in the Church of Scotland after 1610. He was invited to Bangor by the Scottish colonist and county Down landlord James Hamilton, first Viscount Claneboy, who was himself, as we have said, a son of the manse. Blair's account of his ordination and installation in Bangor claims that Echlin, the Bishop of Down and Connor, a Scot who had been ordained by the Presbytery of Dunfermline in 1601, accepted Blair's scruples about episcopacy and liturgy, agreeing to participate in his ordination with some of the neighbouring ministers, coming 'amongst them in no other relation than a presbyter'. Echlin, on the other hand, told the Irish Lords Justices in 1632 that Blair had 'at the time of ordination, no traces of unconformity'. It seems clear that, as so often in situations of compromise, each side had its own interpretation of what was actually happening.

Presbyterian ministers seeking ordination in Church of Ireland parishes in Ulster found the elderly Bishop Knox of Raphoe particularly helpful. John Livingstone of Killinchy claimed that Knox arranged for 'some neighbouring ministers' to join him in ordaining Livingstone in a kind of presbytery ordination. When Knox died in 1634, Archbishop Ussher of Armagh, the Church of Ireland primate, reported that the Raphoe diocese needed 'a bishop who is acquainted with our kind of government' for 'there is not so much as a face of the government of the Church of England'. (sic)

Livingstone, like Blair, was a scholarly man, 'skilled not only in Greek, Latin, Hebrew and Chaldaic' but 'with knowledge of French, Italian, German, Spanish and Dutch'. He was a grand-son of Lord Livingstone who had been one of the guardians of Mary, Queen of Scots. Josiah Welsh, who ministered in Templepatrick, was a grandson of John Knox. Several of the Scottish nonconforming ministers had family connections with some of the leading Scots colonists. James Hamilton, minister of Ballywalter, was a nephew of James Hamilton, Lord Claneboy. Later, Patrick Adair of Cairncastle, the first historian of Presbyterianism in Ireland, was nephew and son-in-law of Sir Robert Adair, a mid-Antrim landlord.

The nonconformity of these ministers did not begin or end with their ambiguous ordinations. Blair had insisted on preach-ing to the Bangor congregation and receiving their 'call' before he would consent to be their minister. A report on the diocese of Down and Connor in 1634 told a story of widespread noncon-formity: 'it would trouble a man to find 12 Prayer Books in all of the diocese', while it was alleged that at communion 'they sit and receive the sacrament together like good fellows'. The Irish Lord Deputy, Sir Thomas Wentworth, observed to the Arch-bishop of Canterbury, William Laud, 'as for bowing at the name of Jesus … they have no more joints in their knees for that than an elephant'.

John Livingstone could claim that in his parish of Killinchy:

not only had we public worship free of any inventions of men, but we had also a tolerable discipline; for after I had been some while amongst them, by the advice of all the heads of families, some ablest for that change were chosen elders to oversee the manners of the rest, and some deacons to gather and distribute the collection. We met every week and such as fell in notorious public scandals were desired to come before us. Such as came we dealt with both in public and private, and prevailed with to confess their scandals be-fore the congregation, at the Saturday sermon before the communion, which was twice in the year, and then were admitted to the communion. Such as after dealing would not come before us or, coming, would not be convinced to confess their faults before the congregation, their names and scandals and impenitency was read out before the congregation, and they debarred from communion, which proved such a terror that we found very few of that sort.

Ecclesiastical discipline was regarded as vital to the life of the Reformed Church. It was the exercise of effective discipline by the Consistory of the Genevan church which had evoked John Knox's famous eulogy of Geneva as:

the most perfect school of Christ that ever was in the earth since the days of the apostles. In other places I confess Christ to be truly preached but manners and religion to be so sincerely reformed, I have not yet seen in any other place.

But not everyone shared the enthusiasm of Knox or Livingstone for the exercise of ecclesiastical discipline. In Bangor Blair was confronted by 'a proud young man, the son and heir of a rich man', who 'falling into scandal proved obstinate', appealing from the congregational kirk session – as the court of minister and elders in a congregation was called – to the bishop 'whereby the order of that discipline was broken'. The youth may have escaped the discipline of the kirk session but, according to Patrick Adair, he did not escape divine punishment: 'God struck that young man a little while after, that he died and a brother, better than he, succeeded him.'

This case of episcopal interference and discipline was but a prelude to increasing confrontation and conflict. It was inevitable, of course, that the compromise which embraced Presbyterianism and Episcopacy within one church, which the Presbyterian historian Scott Pearson called Prescopalianism, would break down when either tradition gained the upper hand.

Two developments hastened that breakdown. A mass movement of religious enthusiasm, known as the Six Mile Water Revival, and led by some of the nonconforming ministers, drew attention to their nonconformity and brought upon them the condemnation of the bishops. Then the arrival in Ireland in 1633 of Sir Thomas Wentworth as Lord Deputy, and his chaplain, John Bramhall, both of whom were committed to the ecclesiastical policies of William Laud, who in the same year had become Archbishop of Canterbury, signalled an end to the official toleration of nonconformity in the Church by law established. Laud's objectives were to encourage the Catholic sacramentarian tradition in Anglicanism and discourage all forms of Puritanism. Theologically he wanted to change the dominant Calvinism of the churches of the Reformation tradition in the United Kingdom, replacing it by Arminianism. Arminianism, like Calvinism and Puritanism, and perhaps even Anglicanism, is a notoriously imprecise term, having different connotations in different circumstances, but essentially it meant the rejection of the Augustinian and Calvinist doctrine of grace, with its emphasis on original sin and the inability of sinful men and women to co-operate with divine grace, for a quasi-Pelagian emphasis on human responsibility and freewill, rejecting predestination in any form beyond foreknowledge. Arminianism was closer to the soteriology of the Council of Trent, which had reacted to the Augustinianism of the Reformers by insisting that men and women, though sinners, could co-operate with divine grace to earn salvation.

In Wentworth and Bramhall, who soon was made Bishop of Derry, Laud had able and energetic agents of his policy. Wentworth was the enemy of nonconformity of any kind in church and state, believing that the foundation of ordered government lay in obedience to lawfully constituted authority, at the head of which was the Crown. He was determined to enforce the authority of the established Church on the one hand, and the obligations of landowners on the other. The nonconformity exemplified in the Six Mile Water Revival was an obvious challenge to episcopal authority in the Church of Ireland and brought to an end the situation of tolerance and compromise.

The Six Mile Water Revival was an early, if not the earliest, example of a phenomenon which was to appear also in Scotland

and colonial America, a movement of popular religious enthusiasm in which nominal church members and godless folk are overwhelmed by a sense of sin and their need of forgiveness. The Six Mile Water Revival followed the earnest preaching of some of the nonconforming ministers in Ulster, described by John Ridge, an English Puritan minister in Antrim, as:

such men for strict walking and abundant pains with their people. Sabbath day, week days, in church and from house to house that I have never known more heavenly in their conversations or more laborious in their ministry.

The Revival, he believed, was a very sweet encouragement for them,

for the Lord hath exceedingly blessed their labours for they have brought a great number of people for twenty miles about them to as great a measure of knowledge and zeal in every good duty as, I think, is to be found again in any part of Christ … Their congregations are, some seven or eight hundred, some a thousand, some fifteen hundred, some more, some less.

The Revival began through the preaching of the 'terrors of the law' by James Glendinning, minister of Oldstone (Templepatrick), which brought conviction of sin to hitherto irreligious settlers, but this eccentric and unstable preacher could not offer the comfort of the gospel to those whose consciences he had awakened. Other ministers, including Robert Blair and John Ridge, of nearby Antrim, and later Josiah Welsh, who succeeded Glendinning in Templepatrick, and John Livingstone, provided responsible teaching, curbing excesses – swooning and shouting – and giving stability and permanence to the revival movement.

To meet the widespread hunger for spiritual nourishment, for word and sacrament, regular monthly meetings for instruction in the faith were organised at Antrim by John Ridge and became known as the Antrim Meetings. Large numbers assembled for a weekend of religious exercises centring on a Sunday communion service, with Saturday as a day of preparation and Monday a day of thanksgiving. Livingstone recorded how he had known people,

to come from several miles from their homes to the communion, to the Saturday sermon and spent the whole Saturday
night in several companies, sometimes a minister being with
them, sometimes themselves in conference and prayers, and
waiting on the public ordinances the whole Sabbath and
spent the Sabbath night likewise, and yet at the Monday sermon not troubled with sleepiness.

Numbers attending were so great that the sacrament was administered in the open air and this and the psychosomatic mani-
festations which sometimes accompanied spiritual experience –
groaning and swooning – evoked criticism from ecclesiastical
authorities, who were, however, reluctant to move against such
popular and effective ministers. Another controversial feature
of the Antrim Meetings was the fact that the ministers involved
gathered to 'consult about such things as concerned the carrying
on the work of God'. These consultations normally preceded the
public meetings and came to be regarded as a kind of proto-
presbytery, another challenge to episcopal authority.

It was bishops in Scotland, however, who initiated the
process which led to the suspension of the nonconforming ministers in Ulster. In 1630 Robert Blair visited Scotland where a
similar revival had been taking place in Ayrshire, in Stewarton
and Irvine, and in Kirk o' Shotts in Lanarkshire, largely as the
result of the preaching of John Livingstone, and was accused of
exciting people to ecstasies and introducing abhorrent Irish
teachings and practices to Scotland. Nonconformity had already
emerged in Scotland and Scottish bishops were endeavouring to
combat radical Presbyterian dissent, privy kirks and private
conventicles. They now demanded that their Irish counterparts
should take action against these disorderly ministers, and in
1631 the Laudian Dean of Down, Henry Leslie, persuaded a reluctant Bishop Echlin to suspend a number of them, including
Blair, Welsh and Livingstone. These were the first of a series of
temporary suspensions, for the nonconforming ministers had
friends in 'high places' and Archbishop Ussher, though no crypto-
Presbyterian as has sometimes been suggested because he was

an ardent Calvinist, was unwilling to drive such men out of the ministry of a church which was struggling to become effective in Ulster. They also retained the loyalty of many of their congregations; during Josiah Welsh's suspension 'his congregation often assembled on the Lord's Day at his house, one of the doors opened into his garden in which the greater number met. In this door he stood and performed the duties of public worship.'

The determination of Wentworth and Bramhall to root out nonconformity in the Church of Ireland and bring it into line with the Laudian Church of England meant that, in 1634, the suspension of the nonconforming ministers became permanent. In that year also the Convocation of the Church of Ireland agreed to adopt the Church of England's Thirty-nine Articles, though Ussher insisted that this did not mean the repeal of the more explicitly Calvinist Irish Articles of 1615, nor would the Church of Ireland accept, without qualification, the 1604 Canons of the Church of England, which prescribed penalties for clergy who did not subscribe the Thirty-nine Articles, the use of the sign of the cross in baptism, bowing at the name of Jesus and a bidding prayer before the sermon. In effect, however, it marked a change of direction and the end of the Calvinist ascendancy in the Church of Ireland.

Rooting out nonconformity in the Church of Ireland was only one aspect of Wentworth's policy of bringing everything in church and state into harmony with the royal will. He endeavoured to increase Crown revenues and recover church lands which were in lay hands. These policies were unpopular in themselves and were made more so by Wentworth's use of the Court of Castle Chamber, modelled on the English Court of Star Chamber, and the ecclesiastical Court of High Commission, all of which contributed to his eventual impeachment in 1640.

In 1634, however, there was no future for men like Blair and Livingstone in the ministry of the Church of Ireland. Clandestine meetings were held in private houses, one centre being the home of Blair's brother-in-law, John Stevenson, an iron smelter who lived near the growing town of Belfast. After negotiations with John Winthrop, Governor of Massachusetts, a decision was taken by a group including Blair and Livingstone to emigrate to colonial America, following the example of the Pilgrim Fathers. But their ship, the *Eagle Wing*, named after the words of the prophet Isaiah, chapter 40, verse 31, 'they shall soar on wings like eagles', probably the first ship to be launched in Belfast Lough, was forced to return after the terrifying experience of two months in the Atlantic. Blair and Livingstone were now among those who returned to Scotland where they were to play leading roles in Scottish Presbyterian resistance to the policies of Charles I and Laud in church and state in Scotland. Livingstone became minister of Stranraer to which some of his former flock travelled to baptisms and communion. Blair, after a brief ministry in Ayr, moved to St Andrews, later becoming Moderator of the General Assembly of the Church of Scotland, after the restoration of Presbyterianism in Scotland.

As in Ireland, Charles I and Laud had been intent upon bringing the Church of Scotland into closer harmony with the Church of England. This involved introducing a Scottish form of the Church of England's *Book of Common Prayer*, erroneously described as 'Laud's Liturgy'. Although the new liturgy was the work of the Scottish bishops, it provoked popular rejection and riot when it was first used in St Giles Cathedral in Edinburgh in July 1637. This marked the beginning of a mass movement of resistance to the autocracy of Charles I in Scotland, with aristocracy, burgesses, churchmen and people uniting to express their resistance in the National Covenant of 1638 condemning recent innovations 'to the ruin of the true Reformed religion, and our Liberties, Laws and States'. A General Assembly, meeting in Glasgow, abolished episcopacy, declared the new *Book of Common Prayer* unlawful, rejected the Five Articles of Perth of 1618 which had restored 'ceremonies' like the sign of the cross in baptism in the Church of Scotland, which now became officially Presbyterian once more. This overturned all that James VI had done to achieve royal control over the church in Scotland and restated classical Presbyterian insistence on the church's freedom from state control. Blair and Livingstone were members of the Glasgow General Assembly.

To Charles I and Laud, the Scottish National Covenant and the acts of the Glasgow General Assembly were 'impertinent and damnable demands', constituting acts of rebellion. Charles was already embroiled in his conflict with parliament in England, which was to lead to civil war, and this inhibited his attempts to use force against the Scottish 'rebels', which ended in victory for the Scots in 1640.

Events in Scotland had important repercussions in Ireland. Wentworth was determined to prevent any movement of support for the Scottish National Covenant by the Ulster Scots. 'We do not want here those who are cordially affected to the Scottish confederacy,' Bramhall reported to Laud, but he could 'praise God that they have neither lords to encourage them and ministers to incite them so I hope we are all secure'. The Scottish nonconforming ministers had been removed and landowners like Claneboy and Montgomery, the leading patrons of nonconforming ministers, who had made their fortunes in Ireland, were in no position to defy the Lord Deputy.

Wentworth now 'persuaded' some settlers to ask for an opportunity to declare their loyalty to the Crown and their repudiation of the Scottish National Covenant. All Scots in Ulster over the age of sixteen were required to take what became known among them as the Black Oath, abjuring the Covenant. Some escaped to Scotland but those who refused to take the oath and failed to escape were liable to savage penalties. Margaret Pont, the wife of Robert Pont, a minister in county Donegal who had denounced episcopacy and fled to Scotland, was imprisoned and heavily fined by the Court of High Commission. Mrs Pont was the daughter of Sir William Stewart, a major landowner, and her treatment may have been a warning to her father who was suspected of Covenanting sympathies.

The number of Scots who had fled from Ulster threatened the viability of the Plantation and became an additional subject of complaint against Wentworth who had made many enemies in

England, as well as Ireland. Sir John Clotworthy, a Devonian with estates in Antrim and Londonderry, became a member of the Westminster parliament where he was closely associated with his relation by marriage, John Pym, who was leading the parliamentary attack on royal autocracy in general and the Irish Lord Deputy's conduct in particular. Allegations that Wentworth, who had become Earl of Strafford in 1640, was building up an Irish Catholic army for use against the king's enemies in Scotland and England, were prominent among the charges which brought about his impeachment and condemnation in 1641.

Clotworthy presented a petition to the Westminster parliament in the name of 'some Protestant inhabitants of the counties Antrim, Down, Derry, Tyrone, etc', complaining about the silencing of 'godly and learned ministers' and their replacement by 'illiterate curates'. While Protestant nonconformity was persecuted, popery was tolerated and even encouraged. The regime

> had been injurious not only to the spiritual but also to the temporal estates of most men, for under the colour of church lands, they have injuriously seized into their hands much of the best land in every county, so that there is scarce a gentleman of any worth whom they have not bereaved of some part of his inheritance.

Such grievances, temporal and spiritual, were calculated to win the sympathy of many members of parliament, who shared the petitioners' antipathy to popery, prelacy and autocratic government, and sympathised with their material loss.

The downfall of Wentworth, and the anti-Catholicism of his and the kings's opponents, increased the anxieties of Irish Catholics, both old English and 'native' Irish. They could see that such toleration as they had enjoyed under Charles and Wentworth was in danger if Charles's enemies triumphed. Thus, when they took up arms in October 1641, they insisted on their loyalty to the king, as of course the Scots had done in their National Covenant of 1638. Indeed there are striking similarities between the oath of association adopted by the Irish Catholics in

Kilkenny in 1642, in the name of the Confederate Catholics of Ireland, and the Scottish National Covenant.

Events in Ireland in 1641 had momentous consequences for Presbyterianism in Ulster. Not only were many Scots settlers and their families killed, contributing to later anti-Catholic mythology, but the rising brought a Scots army to Ulster in 1642 and the chaplains of the regiments of that army formed the first presbytery in Ulster, thus beginning the formal history of Irish Presbyterianism.

CHAPTER 2

Laying The Foundations
of an Irish Presbyterian Church

In spite of the success of the National Covenant, the ensuing victory of Presbyterianism in Scotland and the fall of Wentworth in Ireland, the future of Presbyterianism in Ulster remained bleak in 1641. There were settlers who had Presbyterian sympathies but there was no Presbyterian Church and no real prospect of forming one. The ministers like Blair and Livingstone, who had led the Presbyterian movement within the Episcopal Church of Ireland, had returned to Scotland and were fully occupied in the Presbyterian revolution there. There were no signs that the Church of Scotland felt any responsibility to extend its structures to Ireland to provide for the Scottish *diaspora* there. It was the Irish Catholic uprising of 1641, inspired to some extent by the example of the Scots Presbyters and their successful assertion of their right to their national religious identity, which, ironically, led to the formation of a Presbyterian Church in Ulster. As Patrick Adair, the first historian of Irish Presbyterianism, judged in retrospect, 'the Sovereign Holy Lord in his providence by this rebellion made way for a more full planting of the gospel'. In Adair's view, he had used the rebellion 'for emptying the land of many profane and wicked men, haters of godliness yet under the name of Protestants'. In addition, 'the Irish themselves were greatly wasted by sword and famine so that the land was much emptied of them'.

None of this was apparent in 1641 when it seemed as though the English and Scottish settlements in Ulster would be swept away. Many settlers and their families died and many fled for safety to Scotland or England, though some remained to fight back, with considerable success, against the rebels. In April 1642 the advance guard of a Scottish army, some 3,000 men under the command of Major-General Robert Monroe, arrived in Ulster at Carrickfergus. In August the main army and its commander, Alexander Leslie, Earl of Leven, followed, bringing their numbers up to 10,000 men. The army did not represent, as has often been supposed, a fraternal Scottish intervention to protect the Scots in Ulster. It did come to defeat the Irish rebels but it came under the obligations of a treaty between the English and Scottish parliaments. The Scots army was in English pay, though pay and supplies were to be intermittent and uncertain, forcing the army to 'live off' the settlers, who came to regard it as only a little better than the Irish rebels. While it began by securing counties Antrim and Down, where settler forces were already largely in control, it lost the only major battle fought against the Irish, led by Owen Roe O'Neill, at Benburb in 1646.

Nevertheless the Scots army plays a significant part in our story, because it was chaplains and elders in the regiments of that army who formed the first presbytery on Irish soil on 10 June 1642. It was not, originally, a Presbytery of Ulster but an Army Presbytery providing for the spiritual needs of the army. But when it received as members of presbytery the chaplains of the settler regiments of Lord Claneboy and Montgomery, it had begun to reach out to its host community. Applications to be taken under the care of the presbytery came quickly from a number of parishes which were to become strong centres of Presbyterianism in the future – Antrim, Ballymena, Ballywalter, Cairncastle, Carrickfergus, Comber, Devock, Donaghadee, Holywood, Killyleagh, Larne, Newtownards, Portaferry and Templepatrick. Kirk sessions for pastoral oversight were formed in these parishes. In Adair's words, 'There began a little appearance of a formed church in the country.' While acknowledging the soldiers' lack of piety, he expressed his conviction that 'God made that army instrumental for bringing church government, according to his own institution, to Ireland, especially in the northern parts of it'. Adair, who was one of the first ministers to be ordained and installed by the Army Presbytery, identified the

Presbyterian community with Israel, the people of God, settling in Canaan, surrounded by hostile idolatrous Canaanites, and threatened from within by delinquents among their own people.

We know too little about the continuities and discontinuities between the earlier congregations of Blair and Livingstone, the people who had been affected by the Six Mile Water Revival, and the congregations which now took shape. We do know that one of these who had continued to hold meetings in his own house, and who was now a member of a delegation to the Scottish General Assembly to ask for ministers to be sent to Ulster, was Hugh Campbell who had been converted during the Six Mile Water Revival and in whose home the Antrim Meetings began. Although the Scottish Assembly would not at first allow Church of Scotland ministers to settle permanently in Ulster, which was technically outside the Assembly's jurisdiction, they did send some ministers to Ulster on a temporary basis, among whom were Blair and Livingstone. 'It may be judged,' Adair wrote, 'how refreshful and useful in the country they were, who had been eminently instrumental in laying the first foundation there and for their faithfulness had been driven away ... now they were witnesses of a new reviving and a rising work out of the rubbish.'

Adair acknowledged that the infant Presbyterian Church owed much to new Scots settlers in place of those who had been swept away. He declared that God had 'made way for others who professed the gospel' to come to a land 'overgrown with idolatry and barbarousness'. The parochial structures of the established Church had been largely broken down and Presbyterianism provided new structures such as the kirk sessions, giving leadership in a local community. Although the Scottish General Assembly continued to resist requests for ministers to be allowed to settle permanently in Ulster, the installation of John Drysdale, chaplain to Lord Claneboy's regiment, in Portaferry in December 1642 and James Baty, chaplain to the regiment of Lord Montgomery, in Ballywalter, marked the beginning of settled ministers. Robert Blair gave Drysdale's charge in Portaferry and James Hamilton, who had ministered in Ballywalter from 1626-36, provided continuity with the past. The installations of David Buttle in Ballymena in 1645 and of Archibald Ferguson in Antrim in the same year were followed by a number of ordinations and installations which enabled Patrick Adair, who was ordained and installed in Cairncastle in 1646, to claim, in retrospect:

> ... about this time Providence supplied the defect partly by sending over a new supply of able ministers from Scotland, one year after another by turns, and, thereafter, by sending over divers young men, near together about this time, in 1645 or 1646, besides Mr Ferguson and Mr Buttle, viz. Mr Anthony Shaw to Belfast, Mr Patrick Adair to Cairncastle, Mr Anthony Kennedy to Templepatrick, Mr Thomas Hall to Larne, Mr John Gregg to Carrickfergus, Mr James Kerr to Ballymena, Mr Jeremiah O'Queen or O'Quin to Billy, Mr Gilbert Ramsay to Bangor, Mr Thomas Peebles to Dundonald, Mr James Gordon to Comber, and Mr Andrew Stewart to Donaghadee.

Andrew Stewart was the son of the Rev Andrew Stewart who had ministered in Donegore in county Antrim from 1627 to 1634. Well might Adair

> mark God's wonderful providence in ordering the beginning and foundation of a church here, raised out of the ruin and ashes into which it had been formerly brought, just through the persecution of prelates, and then by a bloody rebellion ... having been but an embryo.

The self-consciousness and identity of the growing Presbyterian community in Ulster had also been stimulated by the circulation and administering of the Solemn League and Covenant. The Covenant was originally a religious statement by the Scottish General Assembly but it became the basis of a political agreement between the Scots and English Parliaments, in opposition to the ecclesiastical and political policies of Charles I. It bound the two parties to preserve and advance the cause of the Reformation in the United Kingdom, to extirpate popery, prelacy and heresy and to secure the rights and liberties of the Scots and English parliaments. The reformation of religion in Ireland was to be one of the cherished aims of the Covenanters.

On 1 April 1644 the Army Presbytery agreed that the Covenant should be administered to the regiments under its care and Adair records that 'in those places where the Covenant was administered to the army the whole country about came and willingly joined themselves to the Covenant', though those who had earlier taken Wentworth's Black Oath were not allowed to take the Covenant until they had 'publicly declared their repentance'. At Carrickfergus 400 men renounced the Black Oath publicly and took the Covenant. Women, as well as men, took the Covenant and, according to Adair, all did so,

> with great affection, partly with sorrow for former judgements and sins and miseries, partly with joy under present consolation, in the hope of laying a foundation for the work of God in the land.

James Seaton Reid, the nineteenth-century Irish Presbyterian historian, considered that the Covenant,

> ascertained and united the friends of civil and religious liberty, and inspired them with fresh confidence in the arduous struggle in which they were engaged. It diffused extensively through the province a strong attachment to the Presbyterian cause. It opened the way for the introduction of the Presbyterian Church into districts where it had previously been opposed, and facilitated its re-establishment in places where it had been violently overthrown. But, what was of still higher moment, the Covenant revived the cause of true religion and piety ... From this period may be dated the commencement of the Second Reformation with which this province has been favoured – a reformation discernible, not only in the rapid increase of churches, and of faithful and zealous ministers, but still more unequivocally manifested in the improving manners and habits of society, and in the growing attention of people to religious duties and ordinances.

Unfortunately, not all could take such a happy view of the administering of the Covenant in Ulster to the settlers. While Adair claimed that 'even some of the Irish' took the Covenant 'with great affection and sincerity', he also reported that some, 'hearing the Covenant was coming that way, fled, because they heard that the Covenant was to extirpate all papists'. Adair's nineteenth-century editor, W. D. Killen, dismisses this as a misunderstanding of the Covenant's purpose to extirpate popery which the Covenanters 'expected to accomplish ... by other means than murdering its professors', but a contemporary American historian of Irish religion and politics, David Miller, comments: 'they had heard, not what the Covenant actually said, but probably what some of the local Protestants believed or wanted it to say'.

The situation in Ulster was changed radically by events in Britain. The agreement of the English parliament to the Solemn League and Covenant in 1643 had raised the hopes of Presbyterians in Ulster and Scotland that Presbyterianism would be established in Britain and Ireland, but the English commitment to Presbyterianism was always equivocal, however. A majority in parliament may have favoured some kind of Presbyterianism but on their own terms. They suspected that full-blown Presbyterianism was another form of clericalism – in Milton's words, 'New Presbyter is but old priest, writ large' – and Erastian Englishmen were not going to surrender their right to order ecclesiastical affairs to clergy of any kind. The Westminster parliament had already agreed to convene 'an assembly of godly and learned divines to be consulted with ... for the settling of church government and vindicating the doctrines of the Church of England from all calumnies and aspersions'. The Solemn League and Covenant was more specific – it pledged its signatories to extirpate popery and prelacy from Britain and Ireland and 'bring the churches in these kingdoms to the nearest conjunction and uniformity in religion, confession of faith, form of church government, directory for public worship and catechizing ... according to the Word of God and the example of the best

Reformed Churches.' For many Scots this meant Presbyterianism, but the English were not so sure. The Assembly of 'godly and learned divines' began their meetings in Westminster Abbey in July 1643 and is known to history as the Westminster Assembly. It was an English body, the eight Scottish commissioners, five ministers and three elders, choosing to adopt an advisory role. To the exasperation of the Scots, a strong Independent lobby emerged in the Assembly. Independents believed that every local congregation should be autonomous, and should not be bound by the diktat of any presbytery, synod or assembly. 'No people had so much need of a Presbyterie', lamented Robert Baillie, the leading Scots commissioner, but the Independents represented a strong constituency in England and, significantly, in the army.

Between 1643 and 1647, the Assembly provided a *Directory for Public Worship*, a *Form of Church Government*, *Larger and Shorter Catechisms* and a *Confession of Faith*, a statement of doctrine published in England in 1648 as *Articles of Christian Religion, approved and passed by both Houses of Parliament*. Authority lay in parliament, not in the Assembly, and parliament made clear, as the magistrates in Calvin's Geneva had made clear a century before, that ecclesiastical actions with social consequences such as excommunication could not be left to churchmen alone, a rejection of the Reformed Church's claim to full spiritual independence. The essence of the formularies is expressed in the answer to the *Shorter Catechism*'s first question: What is man's chief end? Man's chief end is to glorify God and enjoy him forever. *Soli deo gloria.*

Parliament did not have the last word, however. The king, defeated at Naseby in 1645, sought refuge with the Scots but his continuing refusal to accept and subscribe the Covenant led them to hand him back to parliament who were prepared to meet the arrears of pay of the Scots army. But when Charles was seized by the army and taken to the Isle of Wight, a majority in the Scots parliament, feeling that they had betrayed the king, entered into an 'Engagement' with him to support him. A majority in the General Assembly opposed the Engagement, however, because Charles had still not agreed to honour the Covenant. It was therefore the army of a divided nation which invaded England with the ambitious aim of freeing the king, and was defeated at Preston.

The Scots army in Ulster, like Scots in general, was divided over the Engagement, one of the terms of which was that the king would undertake that the army in Ulster should receive its arrears of pay. It was eventually agreed that a substantial force should be sent to Scotland under the command of George Monroe, Robert Monroe's son-in-law, to join the Engagers' invasion of England. In the event Monroe and his men did not reach Preston in time to share in the Scots defeat. They were unable to return to Ulster, however, and the seriously weakened Scots army there was unable to resist the advance of English parliamentary forces under Colonel George Monck. Monck seized Carrickfergus, capturing Robert Monroe who was arrested and dispatched to London, and went on to take the other Scots strongholds, Coleraine and Belfast. Sir Charles Coote, parliamentary commander in the west of the province, took Londonderry. Monck, eager to disarm the suspicions of the Ulster Scots, attended a meeting of presbytery at Lisnegarvey (Lisburn) professing sympathy and support.

Following the defeat of the Scots at Preston, Cromwell had moved against the pro-Presbyterian majority at Westminster who were expelled in December 1648 in what became known as 'Pryde's Purge'. The residual 'Rump' parliament brought Charles I to trial and execution.

The Ulster Presbytery – no longer the Army Presbytery – like the Scottish General Assembly, did not take kindly to the execution of the king or to the ecclesiastical policy of the new regime. On 15 February 1649 the presbytery followed the Scottish Assembly in condemning the execution and calling for the implementation of the Solemn League and Covenant. In *A Necessary Representation of the Present and Eminent Danger to Religion, Laws and Liberties,* the presbytery attacked the proposed

'universal toleration of all religions' as 'an innovation overturn-
ing of unity in religion, and directly repugnant to the Word of
God', encouraging 'damnable errors under the specious pre-
tence of a Gospel-way and New Light'. 'New Light' was always
to be suspect in Ulster Presbyterianism and the presbytery declared its 'utter dislike and detestation of such unwarrantable
practices, directly subventing our Covenant, Religion, Laws and
Liberties'. The *Representation* was to be read to congregations
who were also encouraged to renew the Covenant.

When General Monck transmitted the *Representation* to
Westminster, parliament employed John Milton to draft a reply.
He dismissed the *Representation* as 'a slanderous and seditious
libel, sent abroad by a sort of incendiaries to delude and make
the better way under the cunning and plausible name of a
Presbytery.'

Milton inquired:

Is the Presbytery of Belfast, a small town in Ulster, of so large
an extent that their voices cannot serve to teach duties in the
congregations which they oversee, without spreading and
divulging to all parts far beyond the diocese of Patrick or
Columba, their written Representation, under the subtle pre-
tense of feeding their own flock?

Milton's suspicions of 'the blockish presbyters of Clande-
boye' are confirmed by news just brought and 'too true',

that the Scottish inhabitants of that Province are actually re-
volted and have not only besieged in London-Derry those
forces which were to have fought against the Irish rebels, but
have in a manner declar'd with them and begun open war
against the Parliament; and all this by the incitement and il-
lusions of that unchristian Synagogue at Belfast.

'The Scottish Inhabitants of that Province' had indeed besieged Coote's parliamentary forces in Londonderry. Charles II
had been proclaimed king in Scotland and he was supported by
many Ulster Scots. This brought them into alliance with the
Duke of Ormonde and royalists in Ireland who had also formed
an alliance with the Confederate Catholics who knew that they

had more to hope for in Charles II that from the new regime in England. Monck, finding his position in Ulster untenable, withdrew to Dundalk and entered into a bizarre non-aggression pact with Owen Roe O'Neill.

At this point George Monroe, now Sir George, returned to Ireland commissioned by Charles II to take command of the Scots in Ulster. This caused difficulties since Montgomery of the Ards was already in command and had been recognised by Ormonde. Ormonde did not trust the commitment of the Ulster Scots to the royalist cause, considering that 'that fatal ingredient of the Covenant having still some mixture in it'. He was right. Montgomery and Monroe may have been fighting for the king but many Ulster Presbyterians were committed to the Covenant which Charles had yet to subscribe. Inevitably these differences surfaced and many of Montgomery's soldiers deserted. The Ulster Presbytery, meeting in Bangor on 7 July, condemned Montgomery's lack of commitment to the Covenant and called upon Presbyterians to withdraw from the royalist alliance.

The situation changed totally with the arrival of Cromwell and his Ironsides in August 1649. In a lightning campaign, remembered in Ireland for the massacres at Drogheda and Wexford, he defeated the royalist opposition. Ulster was secured by Coote and Venables for the parliamentary cause. The presbytery may have discouraged support for Monroe and Montgomery but they also held aloof from what Adair called 'the sectarian party'. When they did not respond to Venables' overtures and refused to take an Engagement Oath abjuring Charles II they were outlawed and banished. Charles, having subscribed the Covenant, was crowned king in Scotland on 1 January 1651 but was forced to return to Europe when his invasion of England ended in defeat by Cromwell on 3 September 1651.

Once again the outlook for Presbyterianism in Ireland was bleak. Only six ministers remained in Ulster. Patrick Adair was one of them and he recorded how they continued their ministries as best they could:

Changing their apparel to the habit of countrymen they frequently travelled in their own parishes and sometimes in other places, taking what opportunities they could to preach in the fields or in the barns and glens, and were seldom in their own houses.

To break the link between the Ulster Scots and their mother country a plan was drawn up to transplant them or at least their leaders to the south and west of Ireland. On 23 May 1653 a proclamation ordered 260 Ulster Scots to move from Antrim and Down to Tipperary. Had it been implemented the history of Ireland might have been changed, but it wasn't.

In fact the position of the Ulster Presbyterians improved considerably during the Cromwellian interregnum. In the first place the professed object of the regime to promote gospel preaching in Ireland required effective preachers and these were in short supply. Independent ministers were encouraged to take up the task of evangelisation but there were too few to make much impact outside the garrison towns and, as the infant Church of Ireland had been forced to accept Scots ministers who were Presbyterians by conviction to man the vacant parishes of their church in Ulster earlier in the century, the Cromwellian regime was to find it expedient to allow the Presbyterian ministers who had fled to Scotland to return. They, and some Church of Ireland ministers, were able to officiate as ostensibly Independent ministers in Ireland.

They found particular favour with Cromwell's son Henry who governed Ireland between 1655 and 1659 as, successively, President of the Council, Lord Deputy and Lord Lieutenant. His relations with Presbyterian and former Church of Ireland ministers were often easier than with Baptists, Independents and Quakers. The number of Presbyterian ministers in Ulster grew to between 70 and 80 and, although Presbyterian structures were officially proscribed, they formed what were virtually presbyteries under cover of ministerial associations, gathering for mutual edification and church business. The original Presbytery of Ulster became five 'meetings' of presbytery – Antrim, Down, Route, Laggan and Tyrone. The Synod of Ulster was taking shape.

The origins of Presbyterianism in the south of Ireland belong to this period. These origins, and the early history of Presbyterianism in the south and west of Ireland, still remain to be fully explored. Ulster Presbyterianism, as we have seen, was clearly associated with Scottish immigrants to Ulster and few Scots penetrated the south and west of Ireland. As in Ulster, the first Presbyterians in southern Ireland were within the established Church of Ireland – men like Walter Travers, first resident provost of Trinity College, Dublin and a disciple of Thomas Cartwright, the Presbyterian professor of divinity in Elizabethan Cambridge, who was recommended by Adam Loftus as his successor as Archbishop of Armagh. Scots like James Hamilton and James Fullerton, significant figures in the history of Scots settlements in Ulster, were also involved in the early developments of Trinity as fellows of the College.

During the Cromwellian period a number of Independent and Baptist congregations were formed in Dublin and other urban centres in the south of Ireland. An association of ministers was formed in county Cork as early as 1656 giving concern in governmental circles that it was a kind of presbytery. The Association published its aims and purpose in *The Agreement and Resolutions of Several Associated Ministers in the County of Cork for the Ordaining of Ministers.* The Association was concerned to protect the church from the 'unscriptural intrusion into the work of the ministry' of 'unlearned and unordained' men who were 'causing religion to be despised'. Their aim was 'to walk in the methods of the Westminster Assembly in their advice propounded'.

In 1658 ministers in Dublin and Leinster also formed an Association 'for the furthering of a real and thorough reformation of persons, families and congregations in matters of religion' and they, too, published the terms of their Association. They were clearly Independents in church polity, defining their congregations as consisting of 'persons sound in the faith and of conversation becoming the gospel', but they recognised the value of some kind of union 'though they walk not in all things according to the same rule of church order'. Seymour, a historian of this period in the ecclesiastical history of Ireland, considered that 'it was an attempt to establish a compromise between Presbyterians and Independents, and possibly such Episcopalians as had become "ministers of the Gospel".' They agreed to use The Westminster Confession of Faith, though rejecting 'some points of discipline in the same'. They were to have a Moderator and a clerk and would ordain presbyters though they reserved the right 'to admit any orthodox godly brother who should declare his intention of being regularly ordained as soon as might be'. Unfortunately the names of members of the Association, though apparently attached to the original draft, were not included in the printed copy which has survived.

A number of later Presbyterian congregations have their origins in these Independent and even Baptist congregations of the Cromwellian period. The Presbyterian congregation in Dundalk, for example, originated in the Independent congregation of the Rev Joseph Bowersford, founded in 1650. The first Presbyterian minister of Bandon in county Cork, ordained in 1679, was the son of a Baptist minister. His Baptist congregation in Bandon began its life in the Cromwellian period.

The end of the Cromwellian period found Presbyterians firmly established in Ireland and particularly in Ulster. They shared the conviction of the majority in Britain in favour of the restoration of monarchy and had high hopes for their future under a king who had subscribed the Covenant in 1651. They were prominently represented in the Convention in Dublin which invited Charles II to assume his father's throne. The Rev Samuel Coxe, Presbyterian incumbent of St Catherine's parish in Dublin, was chaplain to the Convention. Charles II was proclaimed king in Dublin on 14 May 1660, six days after his proclamation at Westminster. 'Matters seemed to be on a hopeful course,' observed Adair, but it was soon clear that they had been over optimistic. They should have remembered the biblical maxim to put no trust in princes. An Irish Presbyterian deputation which travelled to London to wait upon Charles were warned to make no reference to the Covenant.

The restoration of the monarchy was followed by the restoration of the established Church. Presbyterians and Independents who had ministered in parish churches in Ireland found themselves facing the painful alternative of conformity or ejection. In January 1661 the Irish Lords Justices forbade all meetings of 'Papists, Presbyterians, Independents and Anabaptists and other fanatical persons', as 'unlawful assemblies'. John Bramhall, who as Bishop of Derry had been a scourge of Presbyterians in the 1630s, returned in 1661 as Archbishop of Armagh, having suffered exile for his Episcopalian principles during the civil war and the interregnum. On his return he was warned by Lord Charlemont that he faced many difficulties, particularly in the north of Ireland, 'abounding with all sorts of licentious persons but those whom we esteem most dangerous are the Presbyterian factions'. Presbyterians who thought of their church as 'ye Church off Ireland', to quote contemporary records of the Antrim meeting of presbytery, posed a special challenge to the established Church as an alternative form of Protestantism, particularly in Ulster. In the main they represented the Scots settler communities, with a congregational kirk session not only enforcing the church's discipline, excommunicating if necessary but, as W. T. Latimer suggested, exercising the function of the later court of petty sessions. Disputes within the community were settled and, as in Calvin's Geneva, it was not only cases of personal delinquency which were dealt with – fornication, adultery, drunkenness – but fraud and dishonesty in business transactions, 'selling drink until people were drunk', or selling drink at the time of worship. The charity of the community, its care of the poor within it, were the responsibility of the session which also linked the congregation with the wider community, through representation in presbytery.

Bramhall, though now a man of sixty-six, quickly began to grapple with the daunting task of re-establishing Anglican structures and worship in Ulster. Twelve new bishops were consecrated in January 1661 in addition to the eight who had survived the interregnum. The most famous of the new bishops was Jeremy Taylor, Bishop of Down and Connor – where Presbyterians were most numerous. Author of such devotional classics as *Holy Living,* he had earlier made a fervent plea for Christian toleration and charity, in his *Liberty of Prophesying,* when his own church was proscribed. 'If persons be Christians in their lives,' he had argued, 'and ... if they acknowledge the eternal Son of God for their Master and Lord, why should I hate such persons whom God loves and who love God?' But now he showed little love for Presbyterians and deprived 36 of their number of their 'liberty of prophesying' in one day.

Presbyterians who had opposed and derided the Cromwellian policy of religious toleration could hardly complain when bishops like Jeremy Taylor did not extend toleration to them. Like Taylor they believed that only true religion should be tolerated. Taylor, according to Adair, 'simply held them not to be ministers, they not being ordained by bishops, and declared their parishes vacant'.

Very few ministers, perhaps seven or eight, conformed. The majority, some 70 in all, chose the costly path of nonconformity. H. C. Waddell, in his tercentenary history of the Route Presbytery, rightly claims that 'the self-sacrifice of these ejected ministers secured the continuance of Presbyterianism in Ireland. Their uncompromising loyalty, under God, saved the Church.' While that is true, it was also the self-sacrifice of the Presbyterian people which secured the continuance of Presbyterianism in Ireland. They had to pay tithes to the established Church and also, in time, to build their own meeting houses and pay their ministers. They became liable to legal penalties for their nonconformity but most of them rejected the ministrations of those who took over the pulpits from which Presbyterian ministers had been ejected. In Kilraughts in county Antrim, the clergyman who arrived to conduct worship on the Sunday after the ejection of the Rev William Cumming in 1662 was faced by an empty church with the carcasses of two sheep suspended from the roof beams.

Mr Cumming had retired to a farm in the parish and continued to minister to his people, visiting them in their homes and holding small gatherings for worship in barns or in the woods. In this he was typical of many of the ejected ministers, as Adair tells us:

> Generally they did reside in some places of their parishes ... They did also, as the danger and difficulty of that time allowed, visit the people from house to house, and sometimes had small meetings of them ... in several places of the parish and in the night-time.

They considered it 'more profitable to their flocks,' Adair continued, to minister in this unobtrusive way, 'without noise or alarming the magistrates and thus continue among their people'.

There were those who wanted to defy the authorities openly as the 'Covenanters' were doing in Scotland. There the division which had emerged in the wake of the Engagement in 1648 had continued and entered a new phase following the Restoration church settlement. As in England, Ireland and Wales, episcopacy had been restored although in Scotland elements of Presbyterianism – kirk sessions and presbyteries in some form – had been allowed to survive under episcopal authority and ministers who had been ordained by presbyteries were not required to undergo episcopal ordination. On these terms a majority of ministers conformed but a minority, swelled when lay patronage was restored and ministers had to obtain, retrospectively, the favour of the patrons of their parishes, resisted. Resistance, involving the formation of alternative, unlawful churches or conventicles, as they were called, was met by repression which, in turn, was met by armed resistance.

The Ulster Presbyterians had been concerned to keep Scottish divisions out of their church in Ireland. The Ulster Presbytery, meeting in Bangor, county Down, in 1654 had accepted an overture, known as the Act of Bangor, binding ministers to refrain from taking sides in current Scottish disputes. Now they resisted fiery Covenanters who opposed the presbytery's quietism. Three young ministers, Michael Bruce of Killinchy, John

Crookshank of Raphoe and Andrew McCormick of Magherally, who had been ejected from their parishes, assembled large gatherings of people whom they excited with passionate preaching in support of the Covenants and against episcopacy. They became marginally implicated in the episode known as Blood's plot, which was to do further damage to the cause of Presbyterianism in Ireland. The traditional account of this episode portrays Blood, a former army officer and small landowner, as leader of an ambitious *coup d'état* involving the seizure of Dublin Castle and risings of opponents of the Restoration Settlement in church and state. Among their aims was 'the establishing of the Protestant religion in purity according to the tenor of the Solemn League and Covenant'. Crookshank and McCormick were alleged to have promised the support of 20,000 Ulster Scots. Blood's brother-in-law, a Presbyterian minister called William Leckey, may have been the real leader of the coup. He was executed while Blood escaped, later to figure in an attempt to steal the crown jewels from the Tower of London, which he also survived, and the abortive coup was used to justify the arrest of Presbyterian ministers in general. None was found guilty, except Leckey, but they were ordered to leave Ireland once more.

Bishop Jeremy Taylor took the opportunity to share his suspicions about the Presbyterians with Ormonde, the Lord Lieutenant: 'as long as those ministers are permitted amongst us there shall be a perpetual seminary of schism and discontent … they are looked on as earnest and zealous parties against the government'. Ormonde later expressed his own opinion, 'that whilst some unconformable silenced ministers are permitted to live in the north the people will never be brought to conformity, and will always be dangerous, and it is certain, though it cannot be judicially proved, that they were active in the contrivance of the late design'. Ormonde hoped that if he could separate the Presbyterian people from their ministers, the people would soon conform, but he soon recognised that this was not so and, before the end of Charles II's reign, he observed that to close meeting houses 'is no better than scattering a flock of crows that will soon assemble again, and possibly it were better to leave them alone than to let them see the impotence of the government upon which they will presume'. In the end the government could not afford to alienate permanently the substantial Ulster Scots population, and Presbyterianism survived.

Archbishop Bramhall died in 1663 and the milder James Margetson who succeeded him was less energetic in leading a crusade against nonconformity. Although most Presbyterian landowners conformed, Presbyterians still had some friends 'in high places', like Lord Massareene, the former Sir John Clotworthy, and some ministers, including Adair, were able to remain as private citizens or chaplains in sympathetic households. One patron of Presbyterianism was major Hugh Montgomery with estates near Maghera who was alleged to have maintained a place of worship for 500 people.

In the end, the 'Blood' episode revealed their political innocence, rather than their guilt, and their position improved, with the result, in Adair's words, that 'the few ministers took every opportunity and made use of any small advantage they had to creep up by degrees to the exercise of their ministry, in their own congregations especially.'

Of course the threat of prosecution for nonconformity still hung over them. Leslie, Bishop of Raphoe, son of Henry Leslie, Bishop of Down and Connor, one of their persecutors in the 1630s, had four ministers in the Laggan arrested, brought before his episcopal court and confined to a house in Lifford for almost six years. He urged his episcopal brethren to follow his example, assuring them that if they did so, Presbyterianism could be extirpated. But they did not and Presbyterianism continued to survive. In April 1669, a minister could report to a friend in Scotland:

> the Lord's work seems to be reviving here. Presbyterians' liberty is, in many places, little less than when they had law for them. They are settling their ministers with encouragement, and building public houses of worship for their meetings ... The harvest is great, the burden bearers are few and the few are not idle.

Lord Robarts, who followed Ormonde as Lord Lieutenant in 1669, was more sympathetic towards Presbyterians and their situation continued to improve. They were now building meeting houses in which they 'performed all ordinances in a public way'. Even presbyteries and kirk sessions resumed meetings and began to enforce discipline in congregations. They benefited from Charles II's Declaration of Indulgence in 1672, which embraced both Catholics and Dissenters, and, in the same year, a royal grant of £600 was made for the support of Presbyterian ministers in Ireland. This *regium donum* or royalty bounty was, and remained, a controversial issue involving, on the one hand, royal support for unlawful ministries and, on the other, exposed the ministers to the charge of being royal hirelings. They were denounced by Covenanting preachers like Alexander Peden who paid visits to Ulster and was well received by many Presbyterians who flocked to hear his prophetic preaching.

The payment of *regium donum* did not free them from episcopal hostility, however. Their increasing activity brought them into conflict with the established Church. In 1673 the Laggan Presbytery ordained William Cox as minister of Clonmel and William Liston as minister of Waterford. Three years later the same presbytery, responding to a request from some Presbyterians in Sligo and Roscommon, sent William Henry of Ballyshannon and Samuel Halliday of Convoy to minister to them. The Bishop of Killala had them arrested and appealed to the Lord Deputy for protection 'from Scotch presbyters who ramble up and down to debauch the people in their religion and loyalty'. It was two years before Henry was brought to trial, when he was released on payment of sureties for future good behaviour. Also in 1673 the presbytery heard that large numbers of their people were being ruined by fines inflicted on them by episcopal courts.

Five years later, the Laggan Presbytery ventured to call its people to a day of prayer and fasting for the church in Britain and Ireland and four of its members were brought before the privy council in Dublin and suffered house arrest for a year when they refused to pay fines of £20 each. One of them,

William Trail, the clerk of the presbytery, told the privy council that the king had no authority 'to set up what government he pleases in the church', but only 'power to set up the one and true government of the church', which, for Trail, meant Presbyterianism.

Trail saw little hope of the true government of the church being established in Ireland and turned his eye towards the new world of promise which was opening up in colonial America. His presbytery had received requests for 'godly ministers', not only in the south and west of Ireland, but from Barbados and Maryland. When, in 1684, a majority of the presbytery's ministers intimated to their brethren in other presbyteries their intention of emigrating 'because of persecutions and general poverty abounding in these parts, and on account of their straits, and no access to their ministry'. Trail had already gone, closely followed by a younger man, Francis Makemie, whose training for the ministry he had supervised, and who had been ordained by the presbytery for service in Maryland. Trail did not remain in America but returned to Scotland and Makemie, who did remain, is honoured as 'the father of American Presbyterianism'.

It was Makemie who formed the first presbytery on American soil in 1706 and this and his fight for liberty to preach in New York when forbidden to do so by the Governor, Lord Cornbury, owed much to his experience in the Laggan Presbytery. There he had learned the value of a presbyterially organised church, to safeguard and propagate the faith, providing nurture, teaching and discipline for its people as they had been provided for him, and the vital importance of religious freedom. His publications in America reveal his attachment to Reformed Christian doctrine as taught in the Westminster formularies and his antipathy to popery, prelacy and the Quakers. The Quakers, like several other radical sects, had appeared in Ireland in the 1650s and hostile references to them in the Laggan Presbytery minutes make clear how Presbyterians regarded them as a serious threat to ordered church life.

We can follow Makemie's training for the ministry in the

presbytery minutes. The first generations of Presbyterian ministers in Ulster had been immigrant Scotsmen, in the main trained
in Scotland, but now the church in Ireland had to supervise and
direct the training of its own ordinands. Makemie's training il-
lustrates the thoroughness with which a presbytery discharged
its responsibilities. In 1672 the Ulster Presbytery's general committee, meeting in Benburb, had drawn up guidelines for ministerial training which had been accepted by all five sub-presbyt-
eries. That training began with general education and, later, involved 'trials' or tests in the biblical languages, Hebrew and
Greek, theological understanding and skill in controversy and
preaching. Makemie matriculated in Glasgow University in
1676, an early pioneer on what became a well-worn path for
Ulster Presbyterian students for the ministry, through Donaghadee and Portpatrick to Glasgow, where they were not always
highly regarded. The process had to begin locally in Ulster, of
course, and many Presbyterian ministers presided over small
grammar schools and classical academies. Attempts to establish
a higher level of education, as in the dissenting academies in
England, never enjoyed permanent success.

One early attempt was made in Antrim, beginning in 1672,
the year in which the guidelines for ministerial training were
adopted. The local Presbyterian minister, Thomas Gowan,
founded 'Antrim Academy' which became a 'philosophical and
divinity school' under the supervision of Gowan and the
English puritan scholar, John Howe, then acting as chaplain in
the household of Lord Massareene. The Laggan Presbytery appointed its own Visitors to the college and agreed to recognise
an education there as the equivalent of 'laureation', or university
graduation. Within two years the Antrim school had collapsed
and a later college in Killyleagh in county Down was also short-
lived. Among its alumni was the famous philosopher, Francis
Hutcheson, who became professor of moral philosophy in
Glasgow University, where his influential teaching made him
one of the early luminaries of the Scottish Enlightenment.

Although the position of Presbyterians in Ireland was far

from comfortable as Charles II's reign drew to its close, they had survived and grown in number in spite of the crises which had put a question mark over their future. But another and final crisis awaited them in the reign of James II. James has been described as having 'all the weakness of his father (Charles I) without his strength'. He lacked the charm of his elder brother (Charles II) and the imagination to foresee the consequences of his actions. His open approval of Catholicism and widespread fear in England that Protestantism might be proscribed and persecuted, following the example of Louis XIV's revocation of the Edict of Nantes in 1685, led to his replacement on the throne by his daughter Mary and her husband William of Orange, champion of European Protestantism.

James turned to Catholic Ireland to enable him to recover his throne with the help of Louis XIV. Thus the 'conflict of the kings' in Ireland was part of a wider European conflict, though it may be simplistic to describe it as a conflict between Protestantism and Catholicism. The Pope was not committed to the cause of Louis XIV though it is not true that William's victory at the Boyne was greeted by a *Te Deum* in Rome.

Irish Presbyterians had little reason to give their lives for the Protestant establishment in Ireland, which had oppressed them as it had their Catholic fellow countrymen. James's Declaration of Indulgence of 1687 had offered a measure of toleration for Dissenters as well as Catholics. The Catholic patriot parliament in Ireland endorsed this policy, promising religious freedom for all, with tithes to be paid to the clergy of one's own church. But Presbyterians' anti-Catholicism was stronger than their antipathy to the established Church of Ireland, and fear of a repetition of the massacres of 1641 led most Ulster Scots to resist James and support William of Orange. Patrick Adair and the Rev John Abernethy of Moneymore went to England in 1689 to lobby William on behalf of the Ulster Presbyterians and express their support.

There was no repetition of the massacres of 1641 but there was considerable suffering. John Abernethy's wife took her children to Derry where she alone survived the siege, though their eldest son, also John, who was to become a leading figure in eighteenth-century Irish Presbyterianism, escaped by travelling to Scotland with relatives whom he had been visiting in Ballymena. Many Ulster Scots fled to Scotland, as in 1641, and Stranraer was again choked with Irish refugees.

The Siege of Derry was to become an enduring symbol of Irish Protestant resistance to the Catholicism of James II but, as in other areas of Irish history, different traditions have conflicting interpretations of the historic siege. Catholic historians have tended to emphasise the weakness of the besiegers who lacked the equipment to breach the walls, while Protestant historians have exalted the heroism of the maiden city's defenders. The Rev George Walker, Church of Ireland hero of the siege, was forced to publish a *Vindication of his True Account of the Siege of Londonderry* in response to the *Narrative of the Siege of Londonderry* by the Rev John Mackenzie, a Presbyterian minister, in which a Presbyterian, Adam Murray, and not Walker, was the hero of the siege.

CHAPTER 3

The Eighteenth Century

1690 may be said to mark the end of the beginning of Irish Presbyterian history. It marked the successful outcome of the last and most serious of the crises which had threatened the future of Presbyterianism in Ireland in the seventeenth century. In the 1690s fresh waves of immigration from Scotland – 10,000 in 1692 alone – augmented and strengthened the Presbyterian presence in Ulster, ensuring its future influence in the province. The Williamite church settlement in Scotland, where the long struggle between Presbyterianism and Episcopacy had ended in the victory of Presbyterianism, was an encouragement for Irish Presbyterians, although there was little prospect of any similar triumph in Ireland. Another encouragement was William's increased *regium donum* grant which was now recognised as an official state payment.

On the second day after the battle of the Boyne, a number of ministers from the different presbyteries met in Belfast to form a Synod of Ulster as a supreme governing body for Ulster Presbyterianism. The original Ulster Presbytery had fulfilled the role of a synod with local 'meetings of presbytery' – Antrim, Down, Route, Laggan and Tyrone – under its umbrella. These meetings had become in effect local presbyteries and the original Presbytery of Ulster had not met since 1661, although in the 1670s representatives of the five 'meetings' had consulted from time to time as a committee to give guidance to the church as a whole. Now the Synod, which met for the first time in Belfast on 26 September 1690, began to meet twice a year and was never driven underground again. From 1693 its meetings became annual. The minutes of some of the early meetings have been lost but we have an unbroken series of minutes from 1697 onwards.

These developments were viewed with concern by the Irish Protestant establishment. There were now five strong Presbyterian congregations in Dublin and in many parts of Ulster Presbyterians predominated. When Jonathan Swift became the incumbent of Kilroot in county Antrim in 1695 he found that a majority of his parishioners were Presbyterians. Like many other members of the Protestant establishment, he came to regard them as a greater threat to the Church of Ireland than the Roman Catholics. Bishop Walkington of Down and Connor fulminated against the Presbyterians in his diocese, exercising 'their jurisdiction openly and with a high hand', holding 'their sessions and provincial synods for regulating all matters of ecclesiastical concern'. Episcopalian landlords were also outraged to find that their influence with their Presbyterian tenants was less than the influence of ministers and kirk sessions.

Earlier attempts to outlaw Presbyterian worship were not repeated but every effort was made to restrict Presbyterian influence and growth. The Irish parliament blocked attempts to have the English Toleration Act of 1689 enacted in Ireland, and in 1704 an Act 'to prevent the further growth of popery' debarred from office all who did not take the sacrament in the Established Church, which included Dissenters as well as Roman Catholics. A tablet in the vestibule of the oldest Presbyterian Church in Londonderry records the names of nine aldermen and fourteen burgesses, a majority in both cases, who forfeited office. In Belfast, Presbyterian burgesses did not resign immediately but in due course were forced to do so. Although the sacramental test was modified by annual Indemnity Acts from 1719 onwards, following the acceptance by Presbyterians of commissions in the militia during the Jacobite crisis of 1715, in breach of the law, it remained on the statute books and as a permanent Presbyterian grievance. Undoubtedly it had a significant effect upon Presbyterian participation in public life and not only in local government. The small number of Presbyterian MPs – nine in 1692 – fell to an average of five throughout the eighteenth century, although there were other MPs like William Connolly, a leading Whig, who were sympathetic to the Dissenting cause. Decline in the political influence of Presbyterians was also due to the fact that many substantial Presbyterian landowners tended to conform. The Upton family of Templepatrick were prominent Presbyterians but when Clotworthy Upton, MP, died in 1725, the new squire of Castle Upton was his brother, John, who had conformed. The defection of Presbyterian landlords like Upton meant an enhanced leadership role for ministers in the Presbyterian community.

Inside and outside the Irish parliament, Presbyterians were attacked as disloyal, turbulent schismatics, a threat to the stability and health of the Irish state. William King, Bishop of Derry, 1690-1703 and Archbishop of Dublin 1703-29, though of Scots Presbyterian origins himself, played a leading part in attacking Presbyterians, opposing concessions of any kind to them. In his *Inventions of Men in the Worship of God* he contended that, contrary to the cherished beliefs of Presbyterians themselves, Presbyterianism was unscriptural in doctrine and worship. The discipline of kirk sessions he castigated as oppressive and tyrannical. He claimed that out of the many Presbyterians in his Derry diocese he had not found any number who knew the Apostles' Creed or the Lord's Prayer. Their sacramental practice was woefully inadequate. In some congregations communion was an annual event and only a minority of the congregations' members communicated or attended public worship. One cannot help wondering how he perceived such a delinquent and ineffective body posing any challenge to the established Church.

Establishment enemies of Presbyterianism were appalled by the grant of *regium donum* for ministerial support. In 1711 the 'Lords Spiritual and Temporal in Parliament assembled', the Irish House of Lords, entreated Queen Anne, whose Tory High Church sympathies were well known to them, to withdraw the Presbyterians' *regium donum*. It was claimed that, in spite of the 'gentle usage' shown to the Presbyterians,

> They have returned us Evil for Good; our Forbearance hath only increased their rage and obstinacy, and by our own lenity

the Northern Presbyterys have been encouraged to seek out and enlarge their Borders. And, not content with the Enjoyment of the free exercise of their religious worship in places where they had settled Meetings, have assumed a Power to send out Missionaries into several places of this kingdom where they have had no call, nor any congregation.

This outreach, it was alleged, was financed by the *regium donum*. The Lords Spiritual and Temporal, as an example of their 'forbearance', directed that a book by Joseph Boyse, 'reflecting on the Legislature and the Episcopal Order', should be burned by the public hangman.

Their appeal to the Queen was ultimately successful and in 1714 *regium donum* was withdrawn, but this triumph was short-lived. Within a year the Hanoverian George I had succeeded Anne and the annual grant was restored and, four years later, was increased to £160, with an additional £400 for 'Protestant Dissenters' in the south of Ireland.

The outreach of Presbyterianism into the south and west of Ireland was particularly resented by the Church of Ireland. By the beginning of the eighteenth century the five Presbyterian congregations in Dublin were flourishing, the Wood Street congregation having 'a thousand hearers on the Lord's Day'. The Rev Alexander Sinclair, minister of the Plunket Street congregation, was Moderator of the Synod of Ulster in 1704. Several leading merchants and aldermen in Dublin were Presbyterians or had some links with Presbyterians.

In 1710 a group of wealthy Dublin Presbyterians established a fund to support and encourage Presbyterianism in the south of Ireland. The fund, which reached a figure of over £7,000, was intended to promote liberty of conscience, the education of students for the ministry and support small congregations. Many Presbyterian congregations in southern Ireland were small, as in urban centres like Cork, Limerick, Bandon, Clonmel, Waterford, Wexford, Sligo and Tipperary. A new and short-lived congregation was established in Galway in 1700. These congregations joined with congregations in Dublin in 1696 to form what was called the Southern Association. As we have seen, the background of most of these congregations was Independent and English rather than Presbyterian and Scottish and they differed from congregations in the Synod of Ulster theologically and in churchmanship. Nevertheless they had what have been described as 'indeterminate and uncertain links' with the Synod of Ulster. Ministers from northern presbyteries were installed in southern congregations and the Dublin 'Presbytery' sent representatives to the Synod of Ulster as 'corresponding members'. In 1710 and 1711 a form of agreement was reached on their relations with the Synod on such matters as ordination of ministers and the exercise of discipline.

In 1726 a new Presbytery of Dublin was formed as a presbytery of the Synod of Ulster, comprising the congregations of Capel Street, Plunket Street and Usher's Quay with Drogheda, Castleblaney, Longford and Breakey. It was the revival of the Presbyterian congregation in Drogheda in 1708 which had provoked the appeal of the Lords Spiritual and Temporal to Queen Anne. Presbyterian ministers preaching in Drogheda were arrested and charged with unlawful assembly though the case against them was ultimately dropped. In December 1712 the Monaghan Presbytery met in Belturbet to 'erect' a congregation there. They too were charged with unlawful assembly and disturbance of the peace. The Irish Lords Justices, one of whom was Archbishop Vessey of Tuam, justifying the prosecution, claimed that 'if such proceedings are not discountenanced, the consequences of them must be the destruction of the English (sic!) Church in this kingdom'. But, once more, the prosecution was dropped on the understanding that the proposed Presbyterian meeting-house in Belturbet would be built at least a mile outside the town. Presbyterians often found some difficulty in obtaining sites for their meeting-houses. That is why some of the older urban Presbyterian church buildings are found at some distance from the centre of the town which they were intended to serve.

Another area of potential Presbyterian expansion, among the native Irish-speaking population, also gave concern to the established Church. In 1712 a Church of Ireland clergyman, John Richardson, published a pamphlet reviewing the history of attempts that had been made 'to convert the popish natives of Ireland to the established religion.' He reported that the Presbyterians were having some success in converting Roman Catholics through preaching to them in Irish and warned that 'if the Established Church does not use the same methods then there will be a great increase of converts to Presbyterianism.'

Richardson exaggerated the achievement of Irish-speaking Presbyterian preachers, however. In 1699 the Dublin Presbytery had asked the Synod of Ulster to appoint 'one or two of their number to preach in the Irish tongue' to assist them in outreach to the native Irish. The Synod responded positively but the project never got off the ground. In 1710, the year in which the Dublin Presbytery established its fund to aid struggling congregations in the south and west of Ireland, the Synod received an overture 'for promoting the gospel through this kingdom among the Irish papists' and resolved 'to imploy some ministers to preach to the Irish.'

They were 'rather encouraged to this because it hath formerly pleased God to countenance such charitable endeavours of our ministers with remarkable success, particularly in the Instances of the Rev Gabriel Corwall and Mr Jeremy Aquin.' Aquin, O'Quin or O'Cuinn, was the first native Irishman to become a Presbyterian minister, licensed by the Army Presbytery in 1646 and ordained at Billy (modern Bushmills). O'Cuinn was a Templepatrick man and the kirk session minutes of the Templepatrick congregation covering this period 1646-1744, reveal many native Irish names among the membership of the infant Presbyterian congregation. It is clear that O'Cuinn was not alone in finding a spiritual home among the Presbyterians. Many, though not the majority, of the Scots settlers in Ulster in the seventeenth century spoke Gaelic and used Gaelic as their primary language for at least one generation. Gabriel Cornwall, a Scot who succeeded Jeremy O'Cuinn in Billy and ministered there and in Ballywilliam until 1690, was a preacher in Irish.

There were other congregations, like Ballybay in county Monaghan, where there was regular preaching in Irish as late as 1690.

Nevertheless, in spite of this tradition of preaching in Irish, the Synod's resolution of 1710 came to very little. Efforts were made to identify ministers who could preach in Irish and to improve their fluency but in 1715 a report into the state of religion and the causes of its present decay instanced among 'the most useful projects' which had been 'either not at all entertain'd' or 'very faintly pursued', 'the proposal for propagating the gospel among the Irish which was intirely and shamefully dropt'. It surfaced fitfully in the business of the Synod over the next few years and then disappeared. Preaching in Irish did continue in some congregations, notably in Dundalk where John Wilson (1700-1702), Patrick Simpson (1707-26) and later, Andrew Bryson (1786-96) were all prominent preachers in Irish, though an order of Synod in 1716 to set up a charity school in Dundalk 'for teaching to read in Irish', like so many of the resolutions of Synod on the subject of Irish, came to nothing. One positive achievement was the publication in 1719, after considerable delay, of a catechism in colloquial Irish edited by Patrick Simpson.

The Synod's 'Enquiry into the state of religion and the causes of its present decay', identified 'Gross Fundamental Errors in Doctrine' as 'a distinct and very great cause of the Decay in Religion'. Arminianism was specified as 'the first Gross Error that broke in upon the purity of Protestant doctrine'. The Enquiry judged that it had become 'deeply rooted and more universally entertained' and had led on to 'abominable heresies such as Socinianism' (which rejected the Divinity of Christ and the doctrine of the Trinity).

It was now a century since the Dutch Reformed theologian, Arminius, had begun to question the axioms of classical Calvinism, its emphasis on original sin and unconditional election. He followed the Council of Trent in emphasising human responsibility, teaching that man, in spite of his sin, could co-operate with divine grace in his salvation. Orthodox Calvinism had responded by affirming what became known as the Five Points of Calvinism: Total Depravity, Unconditional Election, a limited Atonement (Christ died for the elect only) and the Perseverance or assured salvation of the elect, at the Synod of Dort, 1618-19.

By the end of the seventeenth century, classical Calvinism was in retreat in Britain and Europe before the advance of a liberal and anthropocentric theology. 'Seldom has a reversal of fortune been so complete,' wrote G. R. Cragg in his suggestively titled *From Puritanism to the Age of Reason,* 'within fifty years Calvinism in England fell from a position of immense authority to obscurity and insignificance.' In Cambridge, once a citadel of Calvinism, Platonists like Benjamin Whichcote and John Ray taught that human reason, far from being totally corrupted by sin, was 'the candle of the Lord', a divine gift, and that the essence of religion lay in 'universal charity'. There had been a reaction against the dogmatisms of the post-Reformation period which were believed to have led to conflict and even war, contradicting the benign message of the gospel of love. At the same time, the work of scientists like Isaac Newton was providing a simpler, more rational understanding of the universe, contributing to a new confidence in human reason and a demand for a simpler, more rational theology.

Educated Irish Presbyterians could not remain untouched by these currents of thought which students for the ministry encountered during their studies in Scotland. Officially, the Synod of Ulster, like the Church of Scotland, was committed to the doctrines of the Westminster Confession of Faith. In 1698 the Synod followed the mother church in Scotland in enacting that 'young men when licens'd to preach be obliged to subscribe the Confession of Faith'. Opposition soon came from an articulate minority in the Synod who disapproved of subscription to articles of belief as a test of faith and, later, from some who disapproved of the theology of the Westminster Confession. It was clear, however, that the early opponents of subscription, men like the Reverend Joseph Boyse of Wood Street in Dublin, were orthodox on such fundamental questions as the divinity of Christ for it was Boyse who took the lead in bringing his junior colleague in Wood Street, Thomas Emlyn, before the Dublin Presbytery which condemned his acknowledged Arianism (effectively denying the deity of Christ) and deposed him from the ministry in 1702. Emlyn's defence of his Arian convictions led to his civil condemnation on a charge of blasphemy, a stiff fine and a term of imprisonment.

In the context of the Emlyn case, the Synod of Ulster reaffirmed its subscription legislation in 1705, extending the obligation to subscribe to any who had been licensed but had not yet subscribed. It was also in 1705 that a group of avant garde ministers and laymen began to meet in what was called the Belfast Society, to share and discuss books, sermons and ideas. One of the leaders of this group was John Abernethy, minister of Antrim, and a contemporary in Glasgow of John Simson, later a controversial professor of divinity in the university, who was eventually suspended from his chair by the General Assembly of the Church of Scotland. Some years before his final suspension in 1726, he had been warned by the Assembly 'not to attribute too much to natural reason and the power of corrupt nature to the disparagement of revelation and efficacious divine grace'.

Abernethy, like Simson and the Cambridge Platonists, had a high view of 'natural' reason, and was critical of ecclesiastical authority in general and the imposition of doctrinal tests of faith in particular. In 1719 he published a sermon which had originally been read to the Belfast Society entitled, 'Religious Obedience founded on Personal Persuasion', based on Romans 15:5: 'Let every man be fully persuaded in his own mind.' It was a reasoned appeal for liberty of conscience – Christian doctrines could never be imposed by ecclesiastical authority, they could only be accepted by personal conviction.

The sermon excited controversy and an older minister, the Rev John Malcolme of Dunmurry, accused Abernethy and his associates of 'pretending to give new light to the world by putting personal persuasion in the room of church government and discipline'. Thus Abernethy and those who thought like him became known as 'New Lights' while their conservative critics were known as 'Old Lights' who held to the traditional Calvinism of Presbyterianism.

The ensuing controversy became quickly focused on the specific issue of subscription to articles of religion as a test of faith. Abernethy had agreed that a Christian should not be required to submit to 'Human Declarations' on any point of faith. The Synod responded irenically with new legislation on subscription, allowing candidates to offer their own statements of belief in place of passages in the Westminster Confession with which they found difficulty, providing that the relevant presbytery was satisfied with their orthodoxy.

This 'Pacific Act', as it was called, failed, however, to resolve the difficulties of those opposed to subscription. What they opposed was subscription to statements of belief of any kind. This was made clear almost immediately when, in July 1720, the Rev Samuel Haliday, at his installation as minister of the First Belfast congregation, refused to subscribe in any form, affirming his belief that the Scriptures of the Old and New Testaments constituted,

> the only rule of revealed religion, a sufficient test of orthodoxy or soundness in faith and to settle all the terms of ministerial and Christian communion to which nothing may be added by any synod, assembly or council whatsoever.

The Haliday case was discussed at the next meeting of Synod, in 1721, when a majority of those present reaffirmed their subscription to the Westminster Confession in terms of the Pacific Act. Twelve ministers, however, including Haliday and Abernethy, refused to subscribe and were subsequently known as the 'Non-Subscribers'. The Synod tried to find a *modus vivendi* by designating the Presbytery of Antrim as a non-subscribing presbytery but, in the following year, the Synod voted by a small majority to expel the Antrim Presbytery. Significantly, the

Synod's decision was determined by the votes of its ruling elder members. Elders tended to be more conservative than ministers, leading Joseph Boyse to complain of 'the dead weight of the ruling elders'.

In their conservatism, the elders reflected the conservatism of members of congregations, particularly in small areas. New Light and non-subscription might be popular in the sophisticated congregations of Dublin, Belfast and urban centres in east Ulster, but not among rural Presbyterians. Dr Ian McBride has documented the correlation between New Light doctrine and wealthier urban congregations, the world of 'polite Presbyterianism'. It was otherwise in small congregations, in mid-Ulster and west of the Bann. The antipathy of many of the Presbyterian laity to the preaching of New Light is vividly illustrated in the well-known story about the young Francis Hutcheson, the later professor of moral philosophy in Glasgow, preaching in his father's congregation in Armagh. A large number of the congregation walked out and an angry elder, meeting Hutcheson's father, explained:

Your silly son Frank has fashed a' the congregation, for he has been babblin' this hoor about a gude and benevolent God, and that the souls of the heathen will gang tae heaven if they follow the licht of their ain consciences. Not a word does the daft boy ken, speer nor say aboot the gude, auld comfortable doctrines of election, reprobation, original sin and faith. Hoots, mon, awa' wi' sic a fellow.

If the faithful could not longer hear 'the gude, auld, comfortable doctrines of election, reprobation original sin and faith' from New Light ministers in the Synod of Ulster, they began to seek them elsewhere. Ninety families left Abernethy's congregation in Antrim, which probably encouraged him to move to Wood Street in Dublin in 1730, to succeed the Rev Joseph Boyse. Scottish Presbyterian Dissenters, Seceders and Covenanters, who had broken away from the Church of Scotland, soon began to form congregations in Ulster and their conservatism was attractive to many Ulster Presbyterians.

The Williamite church settlement in Scotland had failed to satisfy purist Presbyterians. A Presbyterian national church had been established but it was regarded by some as an Erastian edifice lacking in true spiritual independence. Continuing Covenanters saw the settlement as a betrayal of the great seventeenth-century Covenants which, as covenants with God, they believed to be permanently binding. Clearly an uncovenanted king and government had abandoned any intention of establishing Presbyterianism in Britain and Ireland as required, it was believed, by the Solemn League and Covenant of 1643. The settlement was acceptable, however, to a majority in the Church of Scotland in which there were many ministers who had conformed during the Episcopalian ascendancy, who had never shared their brethren's enthusiasm for the Covenants. The small majority who had remained faithful to the Covenants had maintained their testimony in Covenanting societies in Scotland and in Ulster where they had resulted from the ministry of David Houston who died in 1696.

In addition to these continuing Covenanters, there were others in the Church of Scotland who had accepted the Williamite settlement with reluctance but remained uncomfortable within it. Developments in the early eighteenth century increased this discomfort. The union of the Scottish and English parliaments in 1707 left the established Church in Scotland ultimately at the mercy of a legislature in which Presbyterians were a small minority. This was underlined in 1712 when lay patronage, virtually abolished in 1690, was restored in Scotland by Westminster, affirming the rights of lay patrons of parishes to present their own nominees to be the minister of the parish when a vacancy occurred, which infringed the rights of congregations to chose their own ministers. Also in 1712 a toleration act gave legal recognition to an Episcopal Church in Scotland to exist alongside the Church of Scotland.

As in Ulster, theological conservatives in Scotland were becoming concerned about the apparent defection of many in the Church of Scotland from its Calvinist tradition. Although the church remained officially and legally committed to the Westminster formularies, Dr Ian Hazlett has observed, in a recent survey of theological teaching in the University of Glasgow, that 'Older verities were waning as the Enlightenment began to seep through and weaken the dogmatic scaffolding.' Ulsterman Hutcheson, divinity professors John Simson and later William Leechman, have been identified as the 'unapostolic succession' who led the advance of moderatism or 'new light' in Scotland.

The occasion of the first secession from the Church of Scotland was an act of the General Assembly in 1732 tightening up regulations enforcing lay patronage. The vigour with which a popular minister, the Reverend Ebenezer Erskine, protested against this legislation led to his suspension from the ministry, and subsequently he and three other ministers seceded from the Church of Scotland to form the Associate Presbytery in 1733. Erskine declared that 'There is a difference to be made betwixt the established Church of Scotland and the Church of Christ in Scotland for I reckon the last is in great measure driven into the wilderness by the first.' William Wilson, another of the original seceders, who became their first professor of divinity, gave his view of the context of their secession:

> It was not violent intrusions, (patrons 'intruding' ministers in vacant parishes), it was not the Act of 1732, neither was it any other kind of defection, considered abstractly and by themselves upon which the secession was staked, but a complex course of defection, both in doctrine, government and discipline, carried on with a high hand by the present judicatories of this church, justifying themselves in their procedure and refusing to be reclaimed.

The general background of secession in Ireland was similar. There was no lay patronage in Ireland, where Presbyterians were dissenters, but in 1733 the Synod of Ulster had decreed that the successful candidate in a ministerial vacancy should have the support of two-thirds of the congregation, 'and two-thirds are to be reckoned both from number, quality and stipend of the congregation'. 'Two-thirds men and money', as the new regula-

tion was derisively called, offended humbler members of congregations who saw it as giving undue influence to wealthier
members, and introducing a form of lay patronage. This could
have a theological significance, for the better educated, wealthier
members of congregations tended to be more sympathetic to
New Light than their humbler brethren.

Disgruntled Ulster Presbyterians began to invite the Scottish
Seceders to establish congregations in Ireland, the first being at
Lylehill in Co Antrim in 1714. Reasons for the appearance of seceding congregations were rarely simply theological or ecclesiological. A dispute over the letting of a farm was a contributory
cause of subsequent adversarial developments in Lylehill. There
was also dissatisfaction with the Synod's refusal to respond to
local appeals for a new congregation in the area between
Templepatrick and Lisburn. The Seceders were to meet growing
needs for new congregations which the Synod was reluctant to
form, partly, it has been suggested, because new ministers and
congregations meant a further division of the *regium donum*
which was a block grant to the Synod. It is to be remembered,
however, that there were often difficulties in raising the stipend
of the minister in a small or poor congregation and the Synod
was concerned to ensure that a congregation could maintain a
minister. Secession congregations multiplied in south Armagh,
Monaghan and west Down. The fact that almost fifty congregations – some very small – were formed before the end of the
century and 141 by 1840, when the Seceders united with the
Synod of Ulster to form the General Assembly of the
Presbyterian Church in Ireland, is evidence that they met a popular need.

The first presbytery of the Reformed Presbyterian or
Covenanting Church was formed in Scotland in 1743 and the
first Covenanting preachers or mountain men, as they were
called, came to Ulster in 1744. Unlike the Seceders, they had a
presence already in Ulster in the Covenanting societies who
now appealed for 'a faithful minister to dispense gospel ordinances' and the first Ulster Covenanting minister, William

Martin, a county Down man, was ordained in the open air at the Vow, between Ballymoney and Rasharkin, in 1757. When he was joined in his itinerant ministry by Matthew Lynn from county Antrim, they formed a presbytery, but the Covenanters did not multiply as quickly as the Seceders. Martin was one of several ministers to emigrate to America where a still surviving Covenanting Church was established in Pennsylvania. The original Ulster Presbytery collapsed but was reconstructed in 1792 with six ministers serving twelve scattered congregations from Rathfriland in county Down to Letterkenny in county Donegal.

The Seceders and Covenanters offered a warmer, more intense form of worship and spirituality and a more traditional theology and discipline than the congregations of what Dr Ian McBride has called the 'polite Presbyterianism' of Belfast, Dublin and east Ulster. They had the appeal of 'old-time religion', more popular than the cool rationalism of New Light. Lylehill was close to the Six Mile Water where religious revival had erupted a century before and where large numbers gathered, monthly, for what has been called 'a popular three day eucharistic festival'. Such eucharistic festivals or communion seasons were characteristic of Scottish Presbyterianism and, as in the Antrim meetings in seventeenth-century Ulster, were often associated with religious revival. They could have another aspect, however. They were frequently criticised as occasions of popular festivity, rowdy celebration and even drunkenness, as Robert Burns wrote in his Holy Fair:

There's some are fou o' love divine

There's some are fou o' brandy.

L. E. Schmidt has suggested that they represented a Reformed refashioning of traditional popular Catholic festivity centring on the sacrament.

Dr Henry Montgomery, nineteenth-century leader of the non-subscribers, grew up near Lylehill and attended a Sunday school organised by the Secession congregation's first minister, the Rev Isaac Patton. In his 'Outlines of the history of Irish Presbyterianism', published in a series of articles in the *Bible*

Christian in 1847, he recalled the summer communion season in Lyehill:

> At Mr Patton's summer sacrament, several thousands usually congregated: the Meeting House was choked up; two ministers were preaching at opposite ends of the green; tents, for all kinds of refreshments, were erected on sides of the neighbouring highway and drunkenness and folly profaned the day of rest. Crowds of dissolute or thoughtless persons came from Belfast and over a wide circuit of country 'Lyle Fair' was considered a favourable place of amusement.

Mr Patton was understandably scandalised by such behaviour and for a time towards the end of his ministry, which lasted fifty years, he suspended communion services. By then some ministers were trying to bring 'Holy Fairs' to an end. The Rev Samuel Dill, on his first communion Sunday in Donoughmore in county Donegal in 1799, overturned the stalls on the roadside around his church to discourage this unseemly traffic. Some may see these developments as indications of the 'seriousness' and puritanism which was to characterise nineteenth-century or Victorian Irish Presbyterianism.

Whatever popular festivities may have accompanied communion seasons in Irish Presbyterianism, the right to communicate, to share in the Lord's Supper, was a carefully guarded privilege. New communicants were examined on their faith and manner of life. A minute in the session book of the large Connor congregation in county Antrim records how, on 2 November 1716, the minister, Charles Masterton, later minister of the Third Congregation in Belfast and a champion of subscription and orthodoxy, reminded his new communicants of their baptismal covenant which they subscribe in the following terms:

> We whose names are underwritten do solemnly profess our hearty desire to believe in God the Father, the Son and the Holy Ghost according to the several articles of the Christian faith as they are contained in the Holy Scriptures of the Old and New Testament, summed up in our Confession of Faith and Shorter and Larger Catechisms, and, earnestly desiring

to repent of all our sins we give ourselves up to God the Father ... and to Jesus Christ as our only Saviour and to the Holy Ghost as our Sanctifier ... we promise through grace in all things to behave ourselves orderly and according to the principles we have now professed and that we will deny ourselves and take up our cross and follow Christ as the captain of our salvation until death in the earnest hope of living with Him in endless glory.

Questions might be asked about how much the new communicants understood of what they subscribed but they had been carefully instructed by their minister and the elder of the district in which they lived, particularly in the Shorter Catechism, which was committed to memory. Undoubtedly this instruction in Reformed orthodoxy inclined many church members towards suspicion of those who offered 'New Light'.

It was not only new communicants whose faith and lifestyle were carefully examined; the distribution of the lead communion tokens which gave admission to the Lord's table was never a mere formality – as it often is today – nor was the privilege of having one's children baptised. Elders were expected to question all communicants and parents of children to be baptised about what they believed and how they lived. Did they have family worship, did they and their families keep the Sabbath, did they practise private prayer and teach their children to pray?

Naturally there were many within the family of the church who did none of these things and offended against accepted Christian morality. The exercise of discipline by the kirk session, one of the characteristics of the life of reformed churches, is a subject often clouded by misrepresentation and caricature. Discipline – 'the very sinews of religion', in John Calvin's view – was simply the church's attempt to ensure that what was professed was practised. If sexual delinquencies and sabbath breaking figured largely in the cases dealt with by kirk sessions, that may have been because they were easier to detect and condemn. If some sessions were judgemental and Pharisaical, many obeyed the spirit of Calvin's intention that offenders were to be encouraged and dealt with gently and paternally. Discipline was meant to be redemptive rather than punitive but enforcement of discipline by kirk sessions helped to deprive the Presbyterian Church of some of its remaining members among the gentry. Landlords or their sons could not easily submit to discipline exercised by their tenants in kirk sessions.

Kirk sessions did not only condemn fornicators and sabbath-breakers, they also rebuked those who exploited others and they dispensed sorely needed charity to the handicapped, the widowed and the fatherless.

There were many Presbyterians in eighteenth-century Ulster who needed the charity of their church. Ulster had proved to be no utopia for Scottish immigrants and some of them began to contemplate moving further west, to colonial America, in hope of a better life. It has been estimated that as many as 250,000 Ulster Scots emigrated to colonial America in the half century or so before the outbreak of the American Revolution, in which some of them played leading roles and which was to have a significant impact upon events in Ireland.

Ulster Presbyterian emigrants, beginning with Francis Makemie, had made an important contribution to the development of American Presbyterianism. Makemie organised the first presbytery and in 1716 the first moderator of the first American Synod, John Hampton, was, like Makemie, a product of the Laggan Presbytery. They also contributed to the development of colonial educational institutions, the most famous of which was the Log College at Neshaminy, north of Philadelphia, founded by William Tennent of county Armagh, which evolved into the University of Princeton. Tennent, a graduate of Edinburgh University, had been a minister of the established Church in Ireland who had converted to Presbyterianism in America.

Irish Presbyterians naturally take pride in these achievements but some historians of American Presbyterianism have raised question marks over some aspects of the Ulster Presbyterian contribution which they have seen as divisive. The insistence of some Ulster Presbyterian immigrants on subscription to the Westminster Confession of Faith and their emphasis on the authority of church courts conflicted with the more relaxed outlook of New England Presbyterians and their emphasis on 'experimental' or experiential religion. For them a definite conversion experience was more important than theological or ecclesiological orthodoxy. On the other hand, Francis Makemie related how practical evidence of personal conversion was a necessary qualification for acceptance as a ministerial candidate in the Laggan Presbytery, and the researches of Marilyn Westerkamf have shown that some of the roots of American revivalism are to be found in Ulster soil, in the Six Mile Water Revival on the frontier of the seventeenth-century Ulster colony.

There seems little doubt that some of the Ulster Scots immigrants, like the Scots colonists in seventeenth-century Ulster, were in need of conversion. According to S. E. Ahlstrom, in his *Religious History of the American People,* they 'constituted mainly a mission field.' They were regarded by the Quakers of Philadelphia as an uncouth and pugnacious people, but these characteristics may have made them good frontiersmen, 'troublesome settlers to the government and hard neighbours to the Indians', personified by Davy Crockett, son of immigrants from county Down.

Emigration to colonial America was, of course, one response to the discomforts experienced in Ulster. As Dissenters, Presbyterians suffered a number of religious disabilities, with tithes to pay to the established Church, which claimed jurisdiction in such sensitive areas of life as marriage, education, inheritance and even burial. In his farewell sermon before leading many of his congregation in Aghadowey to emigrate to America in 1718, the Rev James McGregor declared that they were being driven from their farms and families by religious persecution. While not discounting the religious aspect of the emigration movement, recent research has tended to emphasise the pressure of economic circumstances. The Aghadowey congregation was bankrupt and McGregor was owed £80 in arrears of stipend. The local landlord, Richard Jackson, like many other landlords, had raised rents significantly as leases had to be renewed. The rental of thirty-four farms on the Hertford estate near Lisburn was £90-5-6 in 1719; ten years later it was £222-16-7.

Archbishop King, no friend of Presbyterians, protested on their behalf:

> They have already given their bread, their flesh, their butter, their shoes, their stockings, their beds, their house furniture and houses to pay their landlords and taxes. I cannot see how any more can be got from them, except we take away their potatoes and buttermilk, or flog them and sell their skins.

King, who was anxious to blame high rents rather than religious discrimination for the emigration process, anticipated quite remarkably the piteous complaint, later in the century, of the Steelboys of county Antrim:

> betwixt landlords and rectors, the very marrow is screwed out of our bones, and our lives are even become so burdensome to us, by these uncharitable and unreasonable men, that we do not care whether we live or die.

The Steelboys, like the Oakboys of mid-Ulster and the Whiteboys of Munster were agrarian protest movements, spawned, like emigration, by rural discontent. Later in the century this paramilitary underworld would provide foot-soldiers for a movement, inspired by the American and French revolutions, to achieve revolution in Ireland.

Few observers of eighteenth-century Ireland could deny that radical reform, if not revolution, was urgently necessary. In Ireland, as in Western Europe in general, power, wealth and privilege were in the hands of the few, with the many excluded from the decision-making process. But in the eighteenth century questions were beginning to be asked about the old order of hereditary monarchy, ruling aristocracies, state churches and the hierarchical structure of society. Political philosophers, like Ulster Presbyterian Francis Hutcheson of Glasgow University, were teaching their students that governments must be responsible to the people they governed and that the aim of government should be 'the greatest happiness of the greatest number', that, if the rights of the community were trampled upon, the people had the right 'to defend themselves against the abuse of power'.

Such ideas were welcomed by Irish Presbyterians. 'The Presbyterian,' A. T. Q. Stewart has observed, 'is happiest when he is being a radical.' The Calvinist reformation, from which Presbyterianism developed, was characterised by a radical biblicism which rejected hierarchy in church and state, refusing to bow the knee to bishops or popes, kings and emperors. Andrew Melville, chief architect of Presbyterianism in Scotland, had famously told his sovereign, James VI, later James I of the United Kingdom, whom he called 'God's silly vassal', that in the church James was not a king nor a lord nor a head, but a member, 'a subject of King Jesus'. Calvin's Scottish disciple, John Knox, believed that tyrants should be overthrown, if there was no other way of getting rid of them. Presbyterian biblicism meant taking seriously the Bible's concern for political and social justice as articulated by the Hebrew prophets and Mary's Magnificat which has been described as a 'charter of revolution'.

It is not surprising, therefore, to find some Presbyterians supporting enthusiastically the movement for change and reform which emerged originally within the Irish Protestant establishment and the Irish parliament itself, led by lawyers like Henry Grattan and Henry Flood in the Commons and the Duke of Leinster and Lord Charlemont in the Lords. The Protestant establishment had their own grievances. They might seem to exercise unlimited power within Ireland but that power was always subordinate to Westminster and, like the contemporary American colonists, they resented what they believed to be the subordination of Ireland's interests to England's.

The Irish 'Protestant Patriots', as they have been called, and the American colonists, shared a common ideological background in seventeenth-century resistance to monarchical tyranny and the eighteenth-century Enlightenment. Americans used arguments taken from William Molyneaux's *Case for Ireland's Being Bound by Acts of Parliament in England Stated* and Irish patriots drew parallels between the American experience and their own. The American struggle for independence was a model and an inspiration for Irish reformers.

The American war of Independence aided the Irish reform movement in another, more practical way. With British army units withdrawn from Ireland for service in America, Irish national defence required the expansion and reform of the ill-organised and inadequately equipped militia. On St Patrick's Day 1778 some citizens of Belfast formed an independent volunteer company. The Belfast company was the first of many to be formed, first in Ulster and then in the south of Ireland, and within a year more than 50,000 men were in arms. After initial hesitation a suspicious Dublin government gave them official recognition but they always retained something of their original independence, and their alliance with, and support for, the party of reform in parliament contributed to its successes. It was their military muscle which emboldened the Irish parliament to demand and secure from a British government, in the context of the disastrous American war, Ireland's right to freedom of trade and the Irish parliament's freedom to legislate, without control from Westminster.

Many Presbyterians served in the Volunteer companies. Ministers served as chaplains to companies and sometimes as officers. In the words of one of them, the Rev William Steel Dickson, 'the rusty black was exchanged for the glowing scarlet and the title of reverend for that of captain.' Their experience was deeply politicising. In the first place, the sympathy of many Presbyterians were with the American colonists and their cause. A contemporary Presbyterian historian, Dr William Campbell of Armagh, observed that:

> The Presbyterians of Ulster condemned this war as unjust, cruel and detestable. They beheld it with anguish and horror as the most wanton, unprovoked despotism. Their friends and relatives abounded in different provinces of America and they heard with pride that they composed the flower of Washington's army, being carried on by their natural love of liberty.

Volunteer companies were nurseries of political education. Religious exercises gave chaplains, in particular Presbyterian ministers, opportunities to preach radical political sermons, some of which were published. Jemmy Hope, county Antrim Seceder and United Irish leader, recounted in his autobiography how 'his connection with politics began in the ranks of the Volunteers', and that they 'were the means of breaking the first link of the penal chain'. Francis Dobbs, county Antrim landlord and prominent Volunteer leader, complained that 'Every private was taught that he was competent to legislate and consequently to express his sentiments on the most speculative points.' For men like Dobbs the Volunteers had served their purpose and should disappear, leaving the government of the country to parliament. For men like Jemmy Hope the achievements of the Volunteers were a beginning, not an end, of reform.

The parliament which now enjoyed legislative independence remained a conservative and unrepresentative body. Significant reforms had been achieved. Much of the penal legislation against Catholics and Dissenters, including the 1704 Test Act, which excluded Presbyterians from public life, had been repealed, but parliament proved unwilling to grant full civil rights to Catholics or change the unrepresentative character of the legislature itself. Disillusionment with the failure of the constitutional reform movement turned some reformers into revolutionaries and, ultimately, into the rebels of 1798.

As early as 1784 a Presbyterian doctor and radical, William Drennan, another son of the manse, whose father had been a friend of Francis Hutcheson, began to advocate the formation of a secret society on the model of the rapidly multiplying masonic lodges, to plan for what he called 'the complete liberation of the country'. But the Irish Protestant establishment had succeeded in outmanoeuvring and neutering the disunited Volunteers and Drennan's infant revolutionary society remained stillborn.

The French Revolution was to give Irish radicals fresh inspiration and hope. The fall of the Bastille in 1789 was a dramatic symbol of the overthrow of the old order, *l'ancien régime,* a victory

for liberty and progress and was soon being celebrated enthusiastically in Ulster and in Belfast in particular. An increasingly
radical Drennan was soon writing to his friend the Rev William
Bruce, who was also a successor of Drennan's father as minister
of the First Presbyterian congregation in Belfast: 'Reform to be
anything must be revolution. I think that revolutions are not to
be dreaded as such terrible extremes.' Revolution had succeeded
in America and in France, why not in Ireland? To achieve revolution in Ireland, Drennan now believed, required separation
from Britain.

The kind of revolutionary society Drennan had envisaged
emerged in Belfast in 1791 with the formation of the Society of
United Irishmen. It owed its name to a Dublin barrister, Wolfe
Tone, author of an effective *Argument on Behalf of the Catholics of
Ireland* which contended that Irish Protestants had nothing to
lose and much to gain from the concession of full civil rights to
Catholics, who had been invited to Belfast for the inauguration
of the Society. Tone also defined its aims:

> To unite the whole people of Ireland, to substitute the com-
> mon name of Irishman in place of the denominations of
> Protestant and Catholic and Dissenter in order to subvert the
> tyranny of our execrable government, to break the connec-
> tion with England (the never failing source of all our political
> evils) and to assert the independence of my country.

Tone was not a Presbyterian but the committee of that original
Society of United Irishmen were all leading Belfast Presbyterian
radicals: Samuel Neilson, Robert and William Simms, Henry
Haslett, William Tennent and Drennan's brother-in-law, Sam
McTier. Drennan himself was a notable absentee; he had moved
to Dublin where he became chairman of the committee of the
Dublin Society.

1791 was also the year in which shipbuilding began in
Belfast. The foundations of a modern industrial city were being
laid – linen and cotton manufacture, international financial services, a corporation to improve the port and harbour. Economic
advance increased the confidence of the emerging bourgeoisie,

impatient, as elsewhere in Western Europe, with what they saw as archaic and artificial institutions and traditions which retarded progress. They wanted to rationalise and simplify the structures of politics and society, as they welcomed New Light from the pulpits of their churches on Sundays. There is a discernible correlation between radicalism in theology and radicalism in politics. Both have their origins in what the nineteenth-century New Light minister, Dr Henry Montgomery, called 'radicalism of the mind.'

The inauguration of the Society of United Irishmen marked a new stage, a turning-point in the movement for change and reform. The United Irishmen were too radical for some erstwhile reformers. A divisive issue was what came to be known as Catholic Emancipation, full civil rights for Catholics. Some like Henry Joy, proprietor of the *Belfast News Letter* and the Rev William Bruce, argued for gradualism in reform, contending as William Drennan had done earlier, that Irish Catholics were not yet ready for full civil rights. In January 1792 a Belfast town meeting called to consider the Catholic question was divided on the issue of limited or unlimited emancipation. The gradualists were defeated but the division was ominous. A year later, another erstwhile reformer, the Rev Robert Black of Derry, formerly of Dromore, attacked 'seditious spirits who worked to overturn the constitution', warning them that they would be exposed 'to the punishment and infamy due to such atrocious folly'.

Also in 1793 the Synod of Ulster, at its annual meeting, while calling for parliamentary reform and Catholic Emancipation, assuring the Lord Lieutenant that they approved only of constitutional means of obtaining reform, 'rejecting with abhorrence every idea of popular tumult or foreign aid'. Circumstances were to force the United Irishmen to resort to both.

To propagate their radical agenda the United Irishmen founded a newspaper in 1792, the *Northern Star*, to rival and ultimately out circulate the *Belfast News Letter*. Presbyterian ministers, presbyteries and congregations used its columns to call for parliamentary reform and civil rights for all.

On 26 December 1792 the *Star* carried reports of two meetings in Saintfield, county Down. On Christmas Eve the Saintfield Society of United Irishmen had passed a number of resolutions in favour of reform while on Christmas Day the local Presbyterian congregation echoed the same resolutions. The minister of Saintfield, the Rev Thomas Ledlie Birch, was a leading United Irishman.

On 20 February 1793 the *Northern Star* carried an advertisement for a forthcoming publication, *Scripture Politics,* by the Rev William Steel Dickson, minister of Portaferry, comprising three sermons he had preached 'in which the necessity of reform and emancipation were enforced on the basis of Christianity'. Dickson offered an impressive catalogue of biblical texts to show that scripture taught that injustice and abuses of government should be condemned by the church. One of the texts was Isaiah 10:1: 'Woe to those who make unjust laws, to those who issue oppressive decrees to deprive the poor of their rights and withhold justice from the oppressed.' Dickson made it clear that these condemnations applied to the contemporary Irish government:

> Never were partiality and injustice more conspicuous on earth than they have been in the land of our nativity ... Not a small part, but three-fourths of its inhabitants, the great body of the people, have been reduced to the most abject and humiliating servitude, excluded from every office, honour or trust and emolument of the state.

In such circumstances, he declared, 'the nation shall see no prospect of relief and safety but in a radical reform which would remove all these evils – or total revolution'.

Later, another ministerial contributor to the *Star*, the Rev James Porter of Greyabbey, satirised the landlords and aristocracy of county Down in a series of letters which were also published as a popular pamphlet, *Billy Bluff and Squire Firebrand.* Lord Londonderry, of Mount Stewart, near Greyabbey, cannot have enjoyed reading:

> Did you ever see mushrooms in a dunghill? Then you have seen what our new race of lords and earls resemble. They have rotten roots, flimsy stems and spungy heads.

Porter was to pay for his irreverence with his life in 1798.

The situation of the United Irishmen was changed dramatically by the outbreak of war between Britain and revolutionary France in 1798. The government began to take action against those perceived to be 'seditious spirits'. Two prominent Presbyterian United Irishmen, William Drennan and Archibald Hamilton Rowan, the liberal Killyleagh landlord, were charged in 1794 with delivering seditious addresses to Volunteer companies. Drennan was acquitted and became an observer, rather than a participant in the events which culminated in the rebellion of 1798. Rowan was convicted but escaped, first to France, and then to America. In 1795 Tone was allowed to go into exile, first in America but then in France, where he and other United Irishmen were successful in encouraging the French to attack England through Ireland, where, they claimed, a revolutionary situation existed.

The British and Irish governments faced a stark choice of policies in disaffected Ireland – conciliation or coercion. The extension of the franchise to Roman Catholics in 1793 and the provision of Maynooth in 1795 to enable Irish priests to be trained in Ireland, were intended to detach Roman Catholics from the Presbyterian United Irishmen. An increase in *regium donum* for Presbyterian ministers was, in Drennan's view, designed to gag them. The appointment of a liberal whig, Lord Fitzwilliam, as Lord Lieutenant in 1795, indicated a policy of conciliation, for Fitzwilliam was known to favour Catholic emancipation but it was not long before a nervous Westminster government, fearing that he was going too far too fast, surrendered to the Dublin Protestant Ascendancy junta whom he had removed from office, and opted for coercion.

Also in 1795, United Irish hopes of uniting Protestant, Catholic and Dissenter to achieve radical change in Ireland suffered another blow with the emergence in mid-Ulster of the Orange Order as a formidable loyalist and counter-revolutionary force. The roots of Orangeism lay in the Protestant Ascendancy tradition, its anti-popery and veneration for William of

Orange and the Glorious Revolution. In south and mid-Ulster Protestants were confronted by a substantial Catholic popula-tion cherishing memories of a lost Gaelic world and nurturing hopes of reversing their experience of defeat and deprivation. Competition for land and in the domestic textile industry in-creased sectarian tensions. Protestants were alarmed when some Volunteer companies admitted Catholics to their ranks and gave them training in the use of arms. Protestant Peep o'day Boys began to raid Catholic homes, looking for arms and de-stroying the looms of their economic rivals. Catholics responded by joining the Defenders, a Catholic secret society which was spreading in south Ulster and north Leinster, fostering Catholic self-consciousness and confidence. After a pitched battle be-tween Defenders and Protestants at the Diamond in county Armagh in 1795 the Orange Order was founded as a counterpart to the Defenders.

Protestant gentry in county Armagh quickly recognised the value of the Orangemen to defend them and their interests and provided leadership which, for them, had the further advantage of enabling them to recover a measure of control over their un-ruly tenantry. It was the alliance of Protestant gentry and Protestant peasants which gave the Orange Order its distinctive character and strength.

Presbyterian United Irishmen viewed the Orangemen with contempt, as an anachronistic Church and King mob. The *Northern Star* ridiculed them as 'a herd of fellows who adhere to no religious persuasion although they call themselves Protestant Boys', and refused to believe that any Presbyterians were to be found in their ranks. Presbyterians in mid-Ulster, however, did not share the perspective of confident Presbyterians in Belfast and south Antrim and north Down where small Catholic min-orities were not seen as any kind of threat. Some Presbyterians in mid-Ulster were involved in the Order from its beginnings. It was a Presbyterian farmer, James Wilson, from the Dyan in county Tyrone, who was given the honour of holding the war-rant of lodge number one, for the group he led who had been known earlier as the Orange Boys. The nineteenth century Presbyterian historian, W. T. Latimer, considered that 'those Protestants who hated the Catholic more than the landlord became Orangemen, and those who hated the landlord more than the Catholic became United Irishmen'. He claimed that the Presbyterians who became Orangemen belonged to the class of agricultural labourers or country tradesmen who were 'neglected by their ministers because they did not pay stipend', and who sat loosely to the church.

One of the results of the rapid growth of Orangeism was increased Catholic support for the Orangemen's opponents, the Defenders, who became allies of the United Irishmen. The fact that Catholics were driven from their homes in county Armagh at this time gave colour to United Irish propaganda that the Orangemen planned to exterminate Catholics. The United Irishmen have been accused of violating their non-sectarian principles by allying with the Catholic Defenders but recent research has shown that the Defenders were not merely sectarian paramilitaries; they were being politicised and shared the United Irish vision of a social and political revolution in Ireland, though their particular perspective and aspirations were undoubtedly sectarian.

The concentration of Orangemen in mid-Ulster had negative implications for the alliance of United Irishmen and Defenders for they erected a barrier between the United Irishmen of east Ulster and the Defenders of south Ulster and north Leinster. The Orangemen became even more formidable when they were enrolled in the Yeomanry, a new part-time local force raised in 1796 in the context of the war with France intended to take the place of the Volunteers, finally proscribed in 1793. Dungannon MP, William Knox, and his brother General Knox, in command in mid-Ulster, were strong advocates of the formation of the Yeomanry and recruitment of Orangemen as Yeomen. General Knox viewed sectarian strife strategically: 'Upon that animosity,' he declared 'depends the safety of the centre counties of the North'. The Yeomanry in general, however, were not a sectarian force.

The danger of a French invasion in conjunction with risings in Ireland was sharply underscored in December 1796 when a substantial French expedition – ships carrying 15,000 troops with Wolfe Tone in a new role as a French officer – reached Bantry Bay and invasion was only prevented by adverse weather conditions. The screws of the government's coercive policies began to be tightened. Coercion took many ugly forms. In 1797 much of Ulster was placed under marital law enforced by an army described by its commander-in-chief, General Abercromby, as 'formidable to everyone but the enemy'. The contemporary Presbyterian historian, William Campbell, recorded that:

> Fathers and sons were murdered or torn from their families, put to torture, or sent into banishment, without even the form of a trial – their houses burned, their property destroyed and their wives and children left desolate.

The most famous Presbyterian casualty of this period was William Orr, a county Antrim farmer, executed under the 1796 Insurrection Act for allegedly administering the United Irish oath to two soldiers. After a trial judged by many contemporaries to be unsatisfactory, he was condemned to death and, in spite of appeals from many establishment figures, including Lady Londonderry, sister of Lord Camden, the Lord Lieutenant, was executed, declaring on the scaffold, 'I die in the true faith of a Presbyterian.' William Drennan penned a moving epitaph, 'The Wake of Wiliam Orr':

> Truth he spoke and acted truth.
> Countrymen, Unite! he cried
> And died for what his Saviour died.

Remember Orr! was the battle-cry of many county Antrim United Irishmen in 1798.

While the brutal 'pacification' of Ulster forced many to surrender arms and take oaths of loyalty, some even joining the Orange Order to prove their conversion, it goaded others into rebellion. The rebellion when it came in 1798 was disorganised and ill co-ordinated. There was division between those who wanted to await another French invasion and those who wanted to go ahead on their own. The plan, a series of simultaneous risings north and south, hinged on the seizure of Dublin and the rupture of communications between Dublin and the rest of Ireland. But the government forces, well-informed about the United Irish plans, decapitated the Leinster Directory in a pre-emptive strike and the Dublin rising never got off the ground.

The first rising was in Wexford on 31 May but the Wexford men, after spectacular early successes, had been effectively defeated at New Ross on 5 June before the men of county Antrim took the field under the Presbyterian cotton manufacturer, Henry Joy McCracken who had only assumed command on the eve of their attack on the town of Antrim. They in turn had suffered defeat before the rising in county Down on 10 June. Finally, the French did not arrive until August when the main Irish rebellion had been crushed.

Many Presbyterians were involved in the Ulster risings and many were among the casualties both during and after the rebellion, including Henry Joy McCracken. The Synod of Ulster postponed its annual meetings from June until August and embarked on a strategy of damage limitation. It condemned the 'inexcusable crimes of a few members of our body whose conduct we can only view with grief and indignation', and voted £500 for national defence. The contemporary Presbyterian historian, Dr William Campbell, found the Synod's behaviour 'extraordinary'. In its defence it could claim that in 1793 it had expressed its abhorrence of 'popular tumult' and advocated only constitutional means of achieving reform in Ireland but it was surely disingenuous to claim, as it repeated in 1799, that only a comparatively small number had been implicated in 'treasonable and seditious practices'. In his recent research, Dr Ian McBride has identified 63 ministers and licentiates (ministerial probationers) who were suspected of involvement in the rebellion and most of them ministers of the Synod of Ulster.

Only one minister was executed, the Rev James Porter of Greyabbey, and it has been suggested that the inscription on his tombstone should have read 'Murdered by martial law for the crime of writing Billy Bluff'. Two ministerial probationers were also hanged, Archibald Warrick in Kirkcubbin and Robert Goudy of Dunover. The Rev William Steel Dickson was among those imprisoned. Many of those who were implicated in some way went into exile, voluntarily or involuntarily, most of them to America where some had distinguished careers, the Rev John Glendy of Maghera becoming chaplain to the House of Representatives and to the American Senate.

Some nineteenth-century Presbyterians, including the historian, W. D. Killen, claimed that it was largely the New Light non-subscribers who were involved in the rebellion but that is not so. As Ian McBride has written, 'while the New Lights constituted the vanguard of Presbyterian radicalism ... the Enlightenment philosophy of the New Lights cannot explain the mobilisation of thousands of farmers and weavers who "turned out" in June, 1798.'

It is clear that some Presbyterian rebels in 1798 were motivated by a very conservative theological outlook. The Covenanting tradition was stronger in Ulster Presbyterianism than the small numbers of Reformed Presbyterians or Covenanters would suggest. It was nourished by millenarian preaching going back to the seventeenth-century Covenanter, Alexander Peden. A pamphlet circulating in late eighteenth-century Ulster recalled his prophecies that God would use the sword of the French to bring in his kingdom, and the fall of the Bastille was interpreted as a sign of the overthrow of Antichrist. The Covenanting minister, William Staveley, who had ministered to William Orr on the scaffold, provided an introduction to a published sermon entitled *A Discourse on the Rise and Fall of Anti-Christ – wherein the Revolution in France and the Downfall of Monarchy in that kingdom are distinctly pointed out*, in which he observed that 'the millennium state was fast approaching when men will cast off the chains of slavery.' Staveley was imprisoned in 1798 for alleged complicity in the rebellion. Two other Covenanting ministers and two ministerial probationers went into exile. Thus half of the six Covenanting ministers in the Irish Presbytery were suspected of involvement in United Irish activity. Another minister, James McKinney, had already fled to America in 1793, later becoming a vigorous opponent of slavery.

It was not only Covenanting preachers who interpreted contemporary events apocalyptically. Christians of all persuasions from Covenanters to Roman Catholics were influenced by millenarianism, as the revolutions in America and France seemed to signal the end of the Old Order and the dawn of the New. In a sermon preached to the Synod of Ulster in 1793, entitled *The Obligation upon Christians and especially ministers to be exemplary in their lives, particularly at this important period, when the Prophecies are seemingly about to be fulfilled in the Fall of the Anti-Christ*, the Rev T. L. Birch of Saintfield, who was to be imprisoned in 1798 for his alleged part in the rebellion, asked the members of the Synod:

> Have we indeed the distinguished honour of being soldiers to be employed by the Great Captain of our Salvation in that glorious Conflict in which he is finally to defeat the Devil and all his Agents?

It is not surprising that some Ulster Presbyterians saw the rebellion as a crusade to overthrow an uncovenanted king and bring in the kingdom of the Christ of Covenants.

The recent research of David Miller and Ian McBride suggests that numbers of Old Light and New Light ministers suspected of involvement in the rebellion were about equal. Leading New Light figures like Robert Black of Derry and William Bruce of the First Belfast congregation were prominent loyalists while Old Light stalwarts like Henry Henry of Connor and Sinclair Kelburne of the Third Belfast congregation were among those imprisoned in 1798. Presbyterians fought on both sides in 1798. Sir Richard Musgrave, the Tory historian of the rebellion, and no friend of Presbyterians, judged that 'though the Presbyterians lay under a general imputation of being disloyal, it appears that a great portion of them were steadily attached to the constitution, and were ready to draw their swords in its defence.'

Only two Secession ministers were suspected of involvement in the rebellion. It has been suggested that this was because *regium donum* payments had been extended to them in 1784 and they were proving their loyalty. A more creditable explanation may be that the growing evangelical pietism of Seceding ministers inclined them to oppose political utopianism and armed rebellion. In this they were anticipating the alliance of evangelicalism and loyalism in the nineteenth century in Ulster. Their flocks did not always share their ministers' loyalism, however, and the Rev Francis Pringle, Seceding minister of Gilnahirk, on the outskirts of Belfast, made himself so unpopular with his congregation that he had to join his United Irish brethren who were going into exile.

One of the most determined Presbyterian United Irishmen was Jemmy Hope, the Templepatrick weaver who was a member of the Rev Isaac Patton's Secession congregation in Lylehill. Hope survived 1798, in spite of his prominence in the battle of Antrim, and retained his United Irish principles throughout his long life. Many other Presbyterian United Irishmen did not. The disaster of the failed rebellion, the suffering which accompanied and followed it, brought disillusionment and demoralisation. The rebellion, like all armed conflicts, was marked by atrocities on both sides. Lurid reports of massacres of Protestants in the south of Ireland, at Scullabogue and Wexford Bridge, ignoring equally shocking massacres of rebels and their camp followers, were used by loyalist propagandists to persuade Presbyterians that the rebellion in the south was simply a repetition of 1641 and 1689. The recent researches of Kevin Whelan and others have shown that the rebellion in Wexford was not an anti-Protestant crusade led by priests but that was not how it appeared to many Presbyterians in 1798. Even William Drennan commented sadly, 'the savagery of the lower Catholics was greater than the law of retaliation could account for'. The reports of massacres of Protestants in Wexford, the sufferings of United Irishmen and the behaviour of the French at home and abroad completed the disillusionment of many Ulster Presbyterians with the ideology of revolution. The Synod of Ulster, in a pastoral address, told them that the rebellion had been totally unjustified: 'Did not every Christian denomination enjoy perfect liberty of conscience? Were not the shackles broken which had confined our trade? Was not private property secure, and the land every day becoming more prosperous?' James McKey, a loyalist correspondent of Lord Downshire, blamed 'the Presbyterian ministers and rich republican shopkeepers for having led the lower orders into rebellion', and he forecast:

> We will have a much more settled country in a short time than ever your lordship saw it. For some years past there was something brooding in the minds of the republicans and now that it has broke (sic) out, and they could not succeed, they will become loyal subjects.

He was proved right, so far as most Irish Presbyterians were concerned.

CHAPTER 4

The Nineteenth Century:
Outreach at Home and Abroad

Castlereagh, chief architect of the Act of Union, which, in getting rid of the Irish Protestant Ascendancy parliament, achieved one of the aims of the United Irishmen, was determined that Irish Presbyterians should become loyal subjects and supporters of the union. He was advised by his former secretary, Alexander Knox, that,

> This is perhaps a more favourable moment for forming a salutary connection between the government and the Presbyterian body of Ulster than may arrive again. The republicanism of that part of Ireland is checked and repressed by the cruelties of the Roman Catholics in the late rebellion and the despotism of Bonaparte. They are therefore in a humour for acquiescing in the views of government beyond which they ever were or, should the opportunity be missed, may be hereafter.

The means which Castlereagh, guided by Knox and Presbyterian ministers Robert Black and William Bruce, adopted involved a massively increased *regium donum* for ministers, given on new terms. Hitherto *regium donum* had been a block grant given directly to, and administered by, the Synod, and divided equally among its ministers. Under the new arrangements the agent responsible for distributing *regium donum* payments would be appointed and paid by the government, and the Rev Robert Black was given the office. To receive payment each minister must take an oath of loyalty before two magistrates. Black saw to it that William Steel Dickson, released from prison and installed as first minister of a new congregation in county

Armagh, Second Keady, never received *regium donum* again. Another change which many Presbyterians found hard to accept was the classification of congregations by the government according to their size, so that ministers of the larger congregations, placed in the first class, received £100 a year, those in the second class £75 a year and those in the third class £50 a year. There were 62 congregations in each class. Although there were protests against what some saw as the introduction of a hierarchy in a church in which all ministers were considered equal and state interference in the internal affairs of a church which jealously guarded its spiritual independence, the Synod, dominated by the despotic Robert Black, and demoralised in the wake of the rebellion, surrendered tamely.

It is clear from the correspondence of Castlereagh with Knox and Black that their aim was to make Presbyterian ministers, as Knox expressed it:

a subordinate ecclesiastical aristocracy whose feelings must be those of zealous loyalty and whose influence upon their people will be as surely sedative when it should be so, and exciting when it should be so, as it was the direct reverse before.

Presbyterian ministers were to be cast in the role of supporters, rather than critics, of the establishment. A disgusted William Drennan considered that many Presbyterian Church members would abandon Presbyterianism and become Methodists, Independents or Deists. Some did join the Seceders who derided the Synod of Ulster for accepting classification in *regium donum* payments until they themselves accepted the same system in 1810. Only the Reformed Presbyterians or Covenanters remained untainted by government subsidies and they did increase in numbers, forming a Synod in 1811 with twelve ministerial members, whereas there had been only six ministers in the presbytery formed in 1792.

It would be wrong, however, to conclude that the larger number of Presbyterians, the Synod of Ulster and the Seceders, had capitulated totally to the state or that they had all become

Tories and Orangemen. Some undoubtedly did but more remained, as they always had been, radical in their political sympathies. The first trial of strength between the Synod of Ulster
and Castlereagh and the government came with the foundation
of the Belfast Academical Institution in 1810. The Institution was
founded to meet the growing need in rapidly expanding Belfast
for higher education. It proposed to provide a collegiate course
similar to MA courses in Glasgow and Edinburgh and this
naturally appealed to Presbyterians whose ministerial students
had had to go to Scotland for university education. The
Institution promised to meet the long felt need for a college in
Ulster.

Castlereagh and the Tory establishment viewed the Institution
differently. For Castlereagh the Institution, largely the creation
of Belfast's liberal intelligentsia, many of whom had had United
Irish associations, was 'a bastard institution, ostensibly for academical purposes but in reality part of a deep laid scheme again
to bring the Presbyterian synod within the ranks of democracy'.
The fact that William Drennan had given the address at the
opening ceremony in 1814 seemed clear evidence of the political
intentions of its founders and Castlereagh warned Peel, the Irish
chief secretary, of the dangers of allowing 'Dr Drennan and his
associates to have the power of granting or withholding certifi-
cates of qualification for the ministry of that church'.

Both church and college began to feel the weight of government pressure to abandon any prospect of the Institution becoming a training college for Presbyterian ministers. Castlereagh
let the Synod know that the government would look un-
favourably on any such development, hinting that *regium donum*
might not be paid to any minister who was not a university
graduate. The Institution did lose its government grant of £1500
a year when it refused to accept change in its constitution which
would have diminished its independence and brought it more
under government control. The Institution was emphatically
non-sectarian and did not offer teaching in theology, but recognising that students for the ministry in the Presbyterian churches

would be an important section of the anticipated student population of the college, it invited the churches to provide their own divinity professors, whose classes would be accommodated in the college. This became the crunch issue and Robert Black, Castlereagh's spokesman in the Synod of Ulster, threw the considerable weight of his influence and oratory against any such appointment. The Synod, however, asserted its independence and appointed the Rev Samuel Hanna, successor of the Rev Sinclair Kelburn as minister of the Third Belfast congregation, to teach its students for the ministry in the Institution.

The Synod's defiance of Castlereagh was articulated eloquently in a speech by the Rev James Carlile of Mary's Abbey congregation in Dublin:

> Who or what is this Lord Castlereagh, that he should send such a message to the Synod of Ulster? Is he a minister of the body? Is he an elder? ... This day's decision will tell whether we deserve to be ranked as an independent, upright body with no other end in view than the glory of God and the welfare of His church, or whether we deserve that Lord Castlereagh should drive his chariot into the midst of us and tread us down as the offal of the streets.

Castlereagh was unable to persuade Peel to interfere with *regium donum* payments to ministers, Peel arguing that if he had to deal with Drennans he would 'rather have them stipendiaries than independent'. He did not apply this principle to the Institution, which, as we have seen, lost its annual government grant. Thus, in 1817, church and college had stood together for ecclesiastical and academic freedom. The Seceders had earlier taken the same decision and appointed the Rev Samuel Edgar of Ballynahinch as their professor of divinity in the Institution.

Significantly, both professors of divinity, Hanna and Edgar, were evangelicals, and their appointments indicated the growing influence of evangelicalism in Irish Presbyterianism. Evangelicalism had emerged in the eighteenth century as a movement of renewal in Protestant churches from central Europe to the American frontier. Evangelicals emphasised personal religious experience rather than a lifeless confessional orthodoxy. In particular they emphasised and preached the experience of personal assurance of salvation. Churches in Britain, in England, Scotland and Wales, were challenged by evangelicalism and soon British evangelicals were turning their eyes towards Ireland, described by the biographer of the Countess of Huntingdon as 'but little adorned with real evangelical knowledge even in those who assumed the name of Protestants'. The Countess herself, whose daughter married the Earl of Moira, sent some of her preachers to what she infelicitously called, 'poor wicked Ireland'.

A more substantial and influential evangelical presence in Ireland resulted from the evangelism of John Wesley, the first of whose twenty-one visits was in 1747. When he died in 1791 there were some 15,000 members of Methodist societies in Ireland, most of them in Ulster. Presbyterians tended to be suspicious of Wesley's Arminianism and he recorded in his journal that it would be a miracle if there was much fruit from such a dry tree. In time, however, the dry tree did produce fruit and increasing numbers of Presbyterians, ministers and people, experienced the transforming power of the evangelical gospel.

Evangelical advance accelerated in Ulster after 1798, due in part to disillusionment with political utopianism. Patterns of life and the structure of society were being changed by industrial and agricultural revolution, creating new spiritual needs which the cool rationalistic religion of the eighteenth century could no longer satisfy. New Light theology had been attractive to the bourgeois intellectuals of north-east Ulster who, like their counterparts elsewhere in Western Europe, were susceptible to Enlightenment influences and were critical of what they saw as archaic and artificial restrictions on freedom in business, religion and politics. A natural religion, without 'enthusiasm' and mysterious metaphysical dogma, emphasising freedom of opinion and conduct rather than creed, appealed to them. New Light theology flourished in wealthy, urban congregations and not in the frontier situation of mid-Ulster. In the wake of the disaster of the 1798 rebellion, in an unstable and rapidly changing world,

many in all classes were turning to the certainties of evangelicalism and Old Light, rather than the questions of New Light.
As the theologian, John Oman, has observed:

> What Paley's argument could not do, the Evangelical move-
> ment did. It made Christianity level with man as man. And
> what no theology could do, it did. It created a relation to God
> which actually set men free in the midst of the world.

Evangelicalism brought Protestants of different churches together in evangelical outreach. In October 1798 sixteen Seceders,
three ministers of the Synod of Ulster and four from the Church
of Ireland formed the Evangelical Society of Ulster to organise
prayer meetings, Bible and tract distribution and itinerant evangelistic preaching. It was agreed that love should be 'the prevail-
ing principle and all controversies whether political or religious
carefully avoided'; but it proved difficult to avoid such controversies. Evangelical ecumenism fell foul of denominational principles, with the Anti-Burgher Seceders declaring that 'the
Society was not constituted on principles consistent with the
Secession Testimony'. The Burghers were almost equally suspicious and the Society survived for only five years.

Political neutrality was also hard to achieve. In Ireland evangelicalism quickly acquired counter-revolutionary associations.
British and Irish evangelicals regarded the ideology and consequences of the French Revolution as hostile to Christianity. They
appealed for support on the grounds that evangelisation of the
Irish would save Ireland from revolution and rebellion. William
Drennan's sister, Martha McTier, reported on evangelical meetings she had been attending:

> These meetings are held to hundreds in mute attention to a
> variety of well-gifted men of a very superior order and man-
> ner to any itinerants I ever heard, extremely zealous and
> *loyal*, and well fitted for drawing off the people to their *appar-
> ent* purpose, a zealous religion very judiciously blended with
> loyalty and avowing no principle inconsistent with any
> church but that of the new light dissenters.

'A zealous religion judiciously blended with loyalty' was the platform on which the Rev Henry Cooke emerged in the 1820s to lead a campaign against the New Light non-subscribers in the Synod of Ulster. Cooke's leading opponent in the conflict in the Synod, the Rev Henry Montgomery, claimed with some justification that it was Cooke's skill in uniting 'Evangelicism (*sic*) and Orangeism' which was the secret of his popularity and influence, and his success in the conflict in the Synod.

The New Light non-subscribers appeared to have triumphed in Irish Presbyterianism in the eighteenth century. Although subscription to the Westminster Confession of Faith, qualified by the Pacific Act of 1725, remained the law of the Synod, the late J. M. Barkley's researches have shown that 'by the beginning of the nineteenth century more than two thirds of presbyteries evaded the law and admitted candidates without requiring subscription of any kind'. The ethos of the Synod of Ulster was changing, however, as we have seen and what the Presbyterian historian, W. T. Latimer, called 'The Reign of New Light' was about to be challenged.

Subscription to articles of religion did not figure prominently in the agenda of evangelicals, indeed evangelicalism was, in part at least, a protest against a lifeless orthodoxy, but one historian of evangelicalism, W. R. Ward, has observed that 'in most parts of the Protestant world, revival offered some release from the niceties of confessional orthodoxy but in the Highlands (of Scotland) it helped to root them in a popular milieu'. Something similar happened in Ireland. One of the early leaders of evangelicalism in Irish Presbyterianism was Dr Benjamin McDowell of Dublin. He was a herald of things to come when he challenged the non-subscribing élite in the Synod of Ulster in publications like *Regaining Subscriptions to well composed summaries of Christian Doctrine as tests of Orthodoxy* (1770). New Light he derided as Old Darkness, new only in that it was not that knowledge or system of divine truth revealed by the Spirit of God in the Holy Scriptures.

Certainly some evangelicals, including the Rev James Carlile,

Dr McDowell's colleague, were non-subscribers, but they were concerned about Christian doctrine, in particular the doctrine of salvation, which involved questions of Christology. This brought them into collision with some of the non-subscribers who had become Arians, denying the full divinity of Christ. For evangelicals the denial of the full divinity of Christ put a question mark over the Christian doctrines of Incarnation and Atonement. Henry Cooke was echoing Athanasius, the opponent of Arianism in fourth-century Alexandria, when he insisted that 'a Saviour no better or only a little better than ourselves can never be a fit object for the faith, the life, the dependence of sinners'. As Athanasius had argued, only a divine Saviour could save sinful man.

Curiously, it was the Arians, rather than the orthodox, who could be said to have struck the first blow in what became open conflict. It was the invasion of Cooke's Killyleagh parish in 1821 by an English unitarian missionary, John Smethurst, which brought Cooke before the public as a champion of orthodoxy. Cooke was persuaded by one of his elders, Captain Sidney Hamilton Rowan, son of the Killyleagh landlord, the United Irishman Archibald Hamilton Rowan, who was conservative in his theology as his father was liberal, to respond to Smethurst. So enthusiastic was the Killyleagh congregation's response to Cooke's polemics that he pursued Smethurst during the remainder of his preaching tour, attacking his unitarianism.

Later in 1821 a new professor of Hebrew and Greek was appointed in the Belfast Institution. The two leading candidates were the Rev William Bruce, son of the Rev Dr William Bruce, minister of Belfast's First congregation, and the Rev J. R. Bryce, a Seceder. Bruce, like his father, was reputedly an Arian, and Bryce was impeccably orthodox. Bruce was appointed, largely because it was hoped that his father, who had been opposed to the Institution, would change his stance and use his good offices with his friend, Lord Castlereagh, to have the college's government grant restored. Cooke, however, encouraged by one of the Institution's board of management, alleged that Bruce had been appointed because he was an Arian, and that the Institution was becoming 'a seminary of Arianism'. He launched his attack upon Arianism and its influence in the Institution at the annual meeting of the Synod in 1822 and began a campaign to persuade the Synod to demand control over appointments in the Institution, in which teaching of ministerial students was involved, or withdraw their students from the college.

The Institution was deservedly popular in the Presbyterian community who saw no evidence that its students were emerging as Arians and Cooke's campaign to control the college or break the Synod's links with it ended in failure in 1826. In 1827, however, the publication of evidence given to a government commission of inquiry into the affairs of the Institution, gave him an opportunity to attack a number of the Synod's ministers, including the clerk of the Synod, the Rev William Porter, who had acknowledged, on oath, that they were Arians.

When the Synod met in Strabane in 1827, Cooke insisted that a reaffirmation of the church's trinitarian faith was necessary, lest the impression be given that they were all Arians, and, in spite of Henry Montgomery's eloquent appeal for liberty of conscience and the right of private judgement, the overwhelming majority of the Synod's members did affirm their trinitarian faith, thus isolating the small Arian minority. The following year the Synod, meeting in Cookstown, was persuaded to set up a committee to examine the orthodoxy and spiritual experience of future students for the ministry and it was clear that only orthodox and evangelical candidates would be accepted. This led Henry Montgomery and his party, not all of whom were Arians, to publish a *Remonstrance against the proceedings of the Synod*, declaring their intention to secede if their objections were not met and, in 1830, seventeen ministers and their congregations withdrew from the Synod of Ulster to form the Remonstrant Synod which united with the Presbytery of Antrim and the non-subscribers of the Synod of Munster as the Association of Irish Non-Subscribing Presbyterians, later to become the Non-Subscribing Presbyterian Church of Ireland. This loss was balanced, in 1840, by the union of the Synod of Ulster with the Secession Synod to form the General Assembly of the Presbyterian Church in Ireland.

Undoubtedly, as J. E. Davey observed in his centenary history of the General Assembly, the Synod of Ulster, by the Remonstrant schism, 'lost many persons of culture, of wealth, of public spirit and philantrophic zeal'. Many of them were liberals not only in theology but in politics and it has been alleged that the controversy in the Synod was really a political conflict in disguise. Castlereagh, writing to the Prime Minister, Addington, in 1802 had expressed his opinion that it would only be by schism, 'an internal fermentation of the body', that the Synod of Ulster, which had 'partaken so deeply, first of the popular and since of the democratic politics of the country', would 'put on a different temper and acquire better habits'. The schism of 1829-30 has been perceived as the fulfilment of Castlereagh's hopes. Cooke's real objective, John Jamieson, the historian of the Belfast Institution, alleged, was 'the destruction of political liberalism in his church'.

Clearly the conflict in the Synod had political overtones. Henry Montgomery came from a well-to-do county Antrim farming family with United Irish associations, Cooke from the frontier Presbyterianism of county Derry. Only one minister and congregation west of the Bann joined the Remonstrant schism. Montgomery was a public champion of Catholic Emancipation, while Cooke favoured limited emancipation, to preserve the Protestant character of the British state. Cooke therefore drew strength from political partisans who gave him vocal support. He, in turn, made his political sympathies clear. 'We are the determined friends of the British constitution,' he declared in Strabane in 1827, 'we were so in days past when some of those who now oppose us set up the standard of rebellion.'

William Porter, the Synod's Arian clerk, claimed in Strabane that the real reason for attacks upon his Arianism was his advocacy of Catholic Emancipation. Nevertheless it would be wrong to suggest that, in attacking the Arians, Cooke was really ap-

pealing to Presbyterian antipathy to Catholic Emancipation. The
Synod had given its support to emancipation in 1793 and 1813
and when Cooke tried to have a special meeting of Synod called
in 1829 to respond to the imminent concession of emancipation
he was unsuccessful even in his own presbytery. In the year of
his triumph over the Arians in the synod he was defeated on the
question of emancipation.

This was a portent of things to come. If, as Jamieson alleged,
his real objective was the destruction of political liberalism in his
church, he failed completely. While his popularity as the
Athanasius of Irish Presbyterianism was enormous – 'Whenever
he appeared either in the pulpit or on the platform he was sure
to attract an overwhelming audience', reported the historian W.
D. Killen, who was ordained in 1829 – he was never able to command the same sympathy for his political conservatism. Few
Presbyterians approved of his campaign to support the Church
of Ireland when it came under attack in the 1830s from reforming whigs and Catholic O'Connellites. His publication of the
banns of marriage between Presbytery and Prelacy at a great
Protestant and Conservative gathering at Hillsborough in 1834
earned him savage criticism from within his own church.
Clearly there were still ardent political liberals in the Synod of
Ulster after the departure of the Remonstrants. Cooke was still
supporting the Church of Ireland when disestablishment threatened in 1868, but his death-bed appeal to Presbyterian voters to
vote Tory and save the Church of Ireland fell largely on deaf ears.

His unwavering support for Peel and the Tory party, which
the Irish General Assembly held responsible for the disruption
of the Church of Scotland in 1843 over the question of lay patronage in the church, set him at odds with the Assembly which
he refused to attend for several years. Finally, in the 1850s, his
criticisms of the tenant-right movement, and in particular of
Presbyterian ministers sharing platforms with Roman Catholic
priests, threatened to destroy any popularity he still retained.
His position was well described by a liberal opponent, the Rev
A. P. Goudy, grandson of James Porter of Greyabbey:

The Presbyterian Church is laid under a deep debt of gratitude to Dr Cooke. He was made the instrument of accom-
plishing a great reformation in this church by extirpating the
unitarianism which tinged and weakened the body. We shall
never forget the gratitude that is due to him ... But we do not
hold his political opinions on very many subjects. At the
same time we have every reason to believe that our opinions
correspond with a large and increasing majority of Irish
Presbyterians.

One subject on which very many Irish Presbyterians did
share Cooke's political opinions was the union with Britain,
which, like other Irish Protestants, they came to regard as vital
to their interests. The Reform Act of 1832 marked the beginning
of the gradual advance of democracy in Britain, with ever larger
numbers of the population being admitted to the franchise for
parliament with the result that political power began to move
slowly away from large property owners to people in the mass.
It was clear that the Roman Catholics of Ireland, as a majority
population, would become the major political power in the island and Protestants a minority. The union with Britain gave
them the security of knowing that they were part of the majority
population of a great Protestant nation whose ethos and culture
they shared. They became determined opponents, therefore, of
the movement, begun by O'Connell in the 1840s, to have the
union repealed and an Irish parliament restored.

When O'Connell came to Belfast in 1841 to appeal for support for his repeal movement, Cooke challenged him to a public
debate on the issue. O'Connell declined, on the ground that he
did not wish to appear in conflict with the leader of the Ulster
Presbyterians. This was hailed as a great victory for the union
and Cooke achieved new popularity as 'the Cook who dished
Dan'. A great Protestant and Conservative demonstration was
held to celebrate the 'repulse of the Repealer' with Cooke as the
principal speaker. There may not have been too many
Presbyterians among 'the principal nobility, gentry and clergy
of the province of Ulster' present on the occasion, but for once

Cooke enjoyed Presbyterian support for his political stance. Even the liberal Presbyterian newspaper, the *Northern Whig*, normally hostile to Cooke, applauded his challenge to O'Connell.

In Irish Presbyterian historiography the defeat of Arianism in the Synod of Ulster has traditionally been associated with religious revival. W. D. Killen claimed that,

> the attention of the people all over the land was drawn to the great discussion and a marked improvement was everywhere visible. Family prayer revived, sabbath schools increased in numbers and efficiency, new congregations were gathered, churches were rebuilt and repaired and missionary movements were undertaken on a scale never before attempted.

And the Rev James Morgan declared, in his address at Cooke's funeral:

> Our church extension, in the great increase of congregations, our missions, home, foreign, colonial, continental, along with our daily and Sunday schools, our colleges and professors. All these were the issues of the one great measure of which Dr Cooke was the originator.

Certainly Irish Presbyterianism did leap forward after the conflict of the 1820s. In the 1830s eighty-three new congregations were formed although Henry Montgomery alleged that some of them were congregations in name only, owing their existence largely to the government's generous provision of *regium donum* for their ministers. The victory of orthodoxy in the Synod of Ulster and the subsequent restoration of subscription as the law of the Synod in 1835 opened the way for union with the Seceders who had themselves united in 1818 to form a single Secession Synod. 'There can be no shadow of doubt that the schism of the Arians led directly to the union with the Seceders,' wrote J. E. Davey, 'and so to a new age of quickened enthusiasm for the common evangelical inheritance of the Irish churches sprung out of the Scottish Reformation.' The Seceders were now convinced of the General Synod's orthodoxy. The students for the ministry of both synods were being educated together in the

Belfast Institution where they shared in a college prayer meeting and it was they who petitioned their respective synods to consider the question of union. Gradually significant differences were removed – *regium donum* payments were equalised in 1838 and the hated system of classification discontinued. In 1840 the two synods came together to form the General Assembly of the Presbyterian Church in Ireland – 292 ministers and congregations of the Synod of Ulster and 141 ministers and congregations of the Secession Synod. Only a few Secession ministers and congregations remained outside the union, as did the Synod of Munster and their non-subscribing brethren in the north, and the Reformed Presbyterians. Problems remained which have, in some cases, never been solved – two or more Presbyterian congregations in the same village or rural area – but the union was followed by accelerating expansion and development. Many of the agencies and institutions of modern Irish Presbyterianism, missionary, educational and social, had their beginnings in the immediate aftermath of the union, and 137 new congregations were added before the end of the century.

One of the first of the new agencies was the Foreign Mission, inaugurated by the first General Assembly, which commissioned the Rev James Glasgow and the Rev Alexander Kerr for service in India. Earlier Irish Presbyterian missionaries, including the Rev Hope Waddell, Presbyterian apostle to Jamaica and Calabar, had gone abroad under the auspices of the Scottish Missionary Society. The Foreign Mission was quickly followed by a Mission to Jews (1842), a Colonial Mission (1846), to provide a ministry to emigrants to the colonies and, finally, a Continental Mission (1856), to support Protestant minorities in Catholic Europe particularly in Spain and Italy.

The nearest field for Irish Presbyterian outreach, however, was at home in Ireland where there were many, both north and south, who were little better than pagans, whose Christianity was merely nominal. The author of the 'Introductory Remarks' which prefaced the published sermons and speeches delivered at a special meeting of the Synod of Ulster in Dublin in 1833 to consider the Synod's missionary responsibilities asked the question, 'what have the Protestant churches been doing during the last two centuries, for the benefit of the vast population amongst which the Providence of God has placed them?' One of his own answers was that 'the pastors of the Protestant Churches of every name' believed 'that their exertions were to be confined to the people of their own denomination exclusively and that any effort on behalf of the hundreds and thousands perishing for lack of knowledge, outside their own pale, was not to be attempted.'

This is supported by the fact that when the Synod of Ulster did establish a Home Mission in 1826, years after one had been founded by the Secession Synod, any intention of 'interfering with Christians of any other denomination' was specifically disavowed. That changed when the Home Mission united with the Presbyterian Society of Ulster, founded in 1827 'to supply the preaching of the gospel to those deprived of it by an Arian or Socinian ministry' to form the Presbyterian Missionary Society which soon began to promote preaching in Irish to people in the south and west of Ireland.

Presbyterians were relatively late in their participation in Protestant evangelisation in Ireland which had been pioneered in the eighteenth century by evangelists from England like the Moravian John Cennick and the founder of Methodism, John Wesley. In the 1820s William Magee, the Church of Ireland Archbishop of Dublin, appeared to give his approval for what became known as 'the Second Reformation', or more recently 'the Protestant Crusade' in Ireland, when he told a parliamentary committee inquiring into the state of Ireland, 'in respect of Ireland the Reformation may strictly speaking be truly said only now to have begun'. It has been suggested that the real reason for that crusade was not the influence of evangelicalism but the urgent need of the Protestant establishment to convert Roman Catholics if the Protestant Ascendancy, the established Church and even the union were to be secured. There were those like the evangelical Lord Farnham who did think that way but

Presbyterian leaders of evangelical outreach like James Carlile and John Edgar were clearly motivated by spiritual imperatives and social concern. Presbyterians were not part of the Protestant Ascendancy and, as we have seen, were unenthusiastic about saving the established Church.

Dr R. J. Rodgers, historian of Irish Presbyterian outreach to Roman Catholics in the nineteenth century, has judged that,

> Underlying all such missionary activities was a grand, bold, defiant Presbyterian self-confidence. The periodical, the *Irish Presbyterian* spoke of a deep and deliberate conviction that the highest and best interests of Ireland were, and ever had been, associated with Presbyterianism.

'The tendency of our denomination', it claimed,

> is always to develop man's intellectual capacity, foster independence of thought and action, stimulate industry, create in the soul an imperishable love of freedom, a vigorous self-reliance in all the duties and difficulties of life, and, what is better than all, to give prominence and extension to those great living principles of our holy religion, which cannot fail to civilise, purify and elevate mankind.

We may smile at this self-admiring portrait of Presbyterianism but it was rooted in the conviction that Presbyterianism was essentially biblical. Presbyterian self-confidence was confidence in the Bible to bring about reformation in churches, individuals and communities. 'Give me the circulation of the Bible,' declared the Scottish evangelical church leader, Thomas Chalmers, who believed that penal legislation had merely strengthened the attachment of the Irish people to Roman Catholicism, 'and with this mighty engine I will overthrow the tyranny of Anti-Christ and establish the fair and original form of Christianity on its ruins.'

To this end, Bibles were distributed, teachers and schools provided to teach illiterate peasants to read, and Bible readers to explain the Bible to them. Mission stations and, later, Presbyterian congregations, appeared. In 1841 there were 17 Presbyterian congregations in the south and west of Ireland, twenty years later there were 41. The terrible famine of the 1840s, which was felt most acutely in the south and west of Ireland, gave agencies like the Presbyterian mission an opportunity to bring relief and offer spiritual succour. John Edgar's *Cry from Connaught* made clear that it was 'an appeal from a land which fainteth by reason of a famine of bread and of hearing the words of the Lord'. Edgar's sub-title makes clear that it was not only bread for the body but bread of life for the soul which was being offered to a starving population whose fortitude and natural nobility of spirit in affliction Edgar praised.

This invited charges of 'Souperism', defined by Catholic priest, James Maher, uncle of Paul Cullen, successively Archbishop of Armagh and Dublin, as 'holding out relief for the body', in order 'to infect the soul with impious heresies'. In 1848 he wrote to his nephew, then rector of the Irish College in Rome, about Presbyterian success in Connaught:

> They boast of considerable success in the erection of schools and meeting-houses. The famine, they assert, has afforded them many opportunities of impressing upon the poor their views of religion. In truth Presbyterianism is conducted with spirit and activity. The wickedness and uncharitableness of the proselytisers are generally passed over in silence.

Presbyterians like John Edgar and Hamilton Magee, who arrived in Connaught in 1848 to begin a missionary ministry of 50 years, rejected the allegation that they were proselytisers. They insisted that they never sought to make Roman Catholics Presbyterians but only to give them 'living, saving faith in the Son of God'. Edgar told the General Assembly that when he preached in Connaught he simply proclaimed 'the supreme authority of God's Word … justification by free grace, through faith, and the duty of an immediate and unreserved acceptance of Jesus Christ as the all-sufficient and only Saviour'. The professor of theology was surely naïve indeed if he did not recognise that this constituted a challenge to the Roman Catholic Church's understanding and practice of the Christian faith. What were fundamental, basic Christian doctrines to Edgar were 'impious heresies' to Fr James Maher.

While Edgar may have claimed that he advocated 'no prose-lytism in the bad sense, and no bribery' he did recognise that the Famine offered a unique opportunity to win the hearts of Catholics through kindness. This was, of course, a common phil-osophy of mission in the nineteenth century. Cardinal Lavigerie, Archbishop of Algiers and Apostolic Delegate for western Sahara, instructed his White Fathers to love and serve the Africans who would give them their hearts and souls in return. The Presbyterian mission to Connaught did not only offer bread and Bible teaching to a starving population. Industrial schools were established to give instruction in useful skills and a model farm offered teaching in good agricultural practice. Particularly successful for a time were schools for girls in which they were taught sewing, knitting and needlework leading to earnings es-timated at one time as £20,000 a year.

In spite of early successes and advances – six Presbyterian congregations in Connaught became twenty and a break-through seemed to have occurred in Birr in county Offaly, where a Catholic priest and some of his parishioners became Presbyterians – Presbyterian outreach in the south and west of Ireland, like the Protestant crusade in general, ended in ultimate failure. This was due, in part, to Catholic renewal and reorgani-sation. If the Reformation only began in Ireland in the nine-teenth century, the Counter-Reformation followed swiftly and just as the Counter or Catholic Reformation in Europe recovered areas lost to Protestantism in the sixteenth century, so the Irish Counter-Reformation in the nineteenth century responded suc-cessfully to the challenge of the Protestant crusade and before the end of the century Protestantism, including Presbyterianism, was in retreat in the south and west of Ireland. A roofless, win-dowless manse in Ballinglen, where the Rev Michael Brannigan, a convert from Roman Catholicism, had ministered and where the Mission's agricultural school was sited, stood as a stark memorial to Presbyterian defeat.

The Presbyterian mission in the south and west of Ireland may well appear to have been a quixotic exercise. As early as

1828 a Roman Catholic priest told a meeting of the Irish Evangelical Society, 'You might as well attempt to move the earth, as to check the progress of Catholicity in Ireland, and make us all Protestants.' Many individuals, like Michael Brannigan and Philip O'Flaherty, who became a C.M.S. missionary in Uganda, were converted but in 1866 the *Evangelical Witness* conceded that population figures showed that, in Ireland, 'Popery and Protestantism stand relative to each other as they did 30 years ago.'

It may well be that, as the Roman Catholic author of *The Home Mission Unmasked* alleged, numbers of pupils attending schools were inflated by teachers, some of whom were Catholics, to increase their earnings, and that some of the schools scarcely existed. Dr R. J. Rodgers considers that this would 'imply that Ulster Presbyterians were more careless with the distribution of money than has ever been their wont'. His conclusion is that, while some deception may have been involved, it would be absurd to reject all the statistics of teachers and those who inspected the schools as false. The Connaught Mission could never afford extravagance; like the Presbyterian Foreign Mission, it was chronically short of funds.

There was some recognition, by those involved in the Mission, that the Presbyterian presentation of the gospel was too cerebral and intellectual to appeal to illiterate peasants. 'Preaching will not do,' reported one missionary 'for the vast majority could not understand it', and the Rev James Carlile advocated the employment of lay evangelists who could bring down 'the doctrines of salvation more to the level of their capacities than ministers can accomplish'. In a recent essay on Irish Presbyterians and the Famine, the American historian of religion in Ireland, David Miller made the interesting suggestion that 'In targeting the poorest of the poor in Catholic Ireland for conversion in the Famine years, the Presbyterians were seeking to win from the Catholic community the very stratum which they had already lost within their own community.' Famine casualty statistics from Presbyterian ministers in response to a

Dublin Castle inquiry showed that few members of congregations died; those who died came mainly from an underclass who
no longer had any church connection.

The Presbyterian missionaries suffered also from the handi-
cap of being Protestants, associated in the Irish Catholic mind
with what Cardinal Cullen called 'robbery and confiscation of
property'. A new Irish national consciousness was emerging, in
alliance with resurgent Roman Catholicism, which identified
Protestantism with Unionism and Orangeism, with English rule
in Ireland. Missionaries like Hamilton Magee recognised how
much harm was done to their cause by popular Protestant anti-
Catholicism, what he condemned as the 'coarse vulgar and of-
tentimes most ignorant abuse' of 'popery' by Protestants. He
and others tried to acknowledge the sufferings of Catholics, the
injustices to which they had been subjected and to emphasise
how much of traditional Christian doctrine they held in common, but they were swimming against a strong tide.

One result of the Second Reformation or Protestant Crusade
was to sharpen Roman Catholic hostility to Protestantism, thus
undermining the British government's attempts to promote reconciliation and peace in Ireland. To further its ends a reforming
Whig government at Westminster had introduced a national education system to encourage what we today would call integrated
education. The principle on which the system was based was to
be combined secular, and separate religious, education.
Children of all denominations were to be educated together
with religious education forbidden during normal school hours,
after which the clergy of the different churches could instruct
the children of their own denomination. At a stroke this ended
the established church's monopoly of official education which
had been regarded as one of the chief ways of advancing the
cause of Protestantism in Ireland.

Naturally the Church of Ireland resented the loss of their
monopoly of official education which signalled the movement
of the government away from its identification with the cause of
Protestantism, a movement beginning with Catholic Emanc-

ipation in 1829. Catholic response was divided; some, like Archbishop Murray of Dublin, recognising the advantages of the system for Catholics, gave support, while others, like Archbishop MacHale of Tuam, held out determinedly for an exclusively Catholic educational system under the authority of the church. Presbyterians also were divided. The Rev James Carlile of Dublin, like Archbishop Murray, joined the Board of National Education, which administered the system and gave notable service particularly in the field of teacher training. Henry Cooke, on the other hand, led an energetic campaign against the new system, not unlike the campaign he had led against Arianism in his church, alleging that the Bible was being banned from the national schools, in deference to the Roman Catholic Church and that, 'for the first time since the Reformation', Protestants were being required to 'encourage' popery by giving priests access to their schools.

The battle within the Synod of Ulster and between the Synod and the National Education Board was fought for almost a decade, before the government and the Board capitulated to Presbyterian objections and allowed a school at Coreen near Broughshane in county Antrim, whose manager was Cooke's friend and ally, the Rev Robert Stewart, to receive grant aid without agreeing to give access to the school to a Roman Catholic priest. This was a mortal blow against the basic principles of the National Education system and marked the beginning of the end of a brave but perhaps utopian experiment in integrated education, intended to unite Protestant and Roman Catholic in Ireland.

The forces driving Irish Protestant and Catholic apart in the nineteenth century were stronger than attempts to unite them. Both experienced religious revival and this exacerbated rather than moderated their mutual antagonism. Religious revival frequently involves reaffirmation of religious and cultural identities in Ireland. Roman Catholic and Protestant identities were increasingly coming into confrontation and conflict. Desmond Bowen, in *The Protestant Crusade*, the name he gave Protestant

outreach to Roman Catholics in the nineteenth century, describes the division of the people of Ireland after the Union as
two cultures, two identities, the one reflecting 'the traditional alliance with English ways of life', the other, associated with an
ancient Celtic tradition which had been suppressed by the
English conquest. Thus resurgent Roman Catholicism and
Protestant revival reinforced what Bowen calls 'the division of
the peoples'.

Jonathan Bardon, in his *History of Ulster* makes the interesting claim that,

> The Catholic and Protestant revivals were remarkably simi-
> lar in character. Both displayed intense religious fervour and
> a triumphalist assertiveness. Both made faith the cornerstone
> of their beliefs and laid new emphasis on regular prayer, pri-
> vate devotions, participation in church services and Sunday
> instruction for children. Both embraced a fervent puritanism
> and were opposed to sexual permissiveness, strong drink
> and pernicious literature. Both accepted infallibility, one of
> the pope and the other of the literal truth of the Bible as God's
> word.

But it was their differences which exacerbated division. Each
emphasised elements in their traditions which were in conflict
with each other. So the ultramontanist movement in Catholicism
emphasised the authority of the pope, who was declared to be
infallible, the role and place of the Virgin Mary, whose immaculate conception was promulgated, the absolute validity of the
Catholic perspective in every aspect of life, laid down in the
Syllabus of Errors and an increasingly church-centred piety characterised by such new devotions of Roman origin as the rosary,
the forty hours, novenas, devotion to the Sacred Heart and the
Immaculate Conception, pilgrimages, processions and retreats.

Protestant evangelicalism, on the other hand, emphasised
the authority of the Bible and the central Reformation doctrine
of justification by grace through faith, that a man or woman
could be saved and know it without the mediation of priest or
sacrament. The cherished affirmations of one were the de-

testable heresies of the other. In spite of irenical evangelists like Hamilton Magee the obverse side of Presbyterianism was too often anti-Catholicism.

Roman Catholics in Connaught were not the only targets of Presbyterian evangelicals. They were concerned about the unchurched underclass whom David Miller considers they had lost, who found an increasingly middle-class church, with pew rents, bourgeois respectability and long sermons, unattractive. In common with other Protestant churches in Britain and Western Europe, the Irish Presbyterian Church was losing the lowest strata of industrial workers in rapidly growing Belfast. The Belfast Town Mission, founded in 1827, to promote 'Christ's cause among the poor, the careless and the churchless', became an auxiliary of the Presbyterian Church in 1843. The Town, later City, Mission was a monument to the failure of Presbyterian congregations to meet the spiritual needs of many of Belfast's citizens. Indeed the mission halls of one kind or another, which were to become features of the Ulster religious landscape, particularly after the revival of 1859, represented a protest against the mainstream churches and their patterns of worship and ministry.

Town missionaries were not the only evangelists reaching out to the unchurched. Earnest evangelical ministers like the Rev John Johnston of Tullylish and his son William who, as minister of Townsend Street congregation in Belfast, became one of the most influential figures in nineteenth-century Irish Presbyterianism, were pioneers in open-air preaching, which, by the 1850s, was encouraged by the General Assembly. Corporate prayer was also encouraged and prayer meetings were organised in most congregations. When the Rev James Foster, father of the Presbyterian novelist Lydia M. Foster, was ordained in New Mills in county Tyrone in 1850, he 'gave priority to the formation of a network of prayer meetings encircling the congregational area'.

One of the great objects of prayer, whether in prayer meetings or in congregational worship or in the General Assembly was for a 'revival' of religion. The pattern of such revivals had been established in Ulster and the west of Scotland in the early seventeenth century. An American historian, Marilyn Westerkamp, exploring the origins of the eighteenth century Great Awakening in America, found that her researches led her to seventeenth-century Ulster and the Six Mile Water Revival which she describes as 'the first of its kind, at least the first recorded, to rise up in the British Isles'.

And she continues:

Without doubt, over one hundred years before Whitefield began to preach, Ireland experienced its own Awakening. This awakening established traditions of revivalism and enthusiasm, traditions that would inform the course of religious history for the next four centuries.

The Six Mile Water Revival had been largely forgotten by Irish Presbyterians during the reign of New Light in the eighteenth century, but it was recalled vividly in 1828 by the Rev James Seaton Reid, known today as the father of Irish Presbyterian historiography, in a moderatorial address to the Synod of Ulster, subsequently published as *The History of the Presbyterian Church in Ireland, briefly reviewed and practically improved*. Using as his text the words of Rev 11:5, 'Remember therefore from whence thou art fallen', he presented the history of their church as a falling away from a golden age in the seventeenth century when 'the people, who had been proverbially careless and ungodly, became truly religious – delighting in all the ordinances of the gospel, and glorifying their great God and Saviour by their exemplary lives.'

The 'practical improvement' which Reid urged upon the Synod was that they should recover the spiritual vitality of that golden age by making use of the same means which had brought it about in the earlier age:

It is delightful to dwell on the spectacle which our infant church, though confined to a very limited sphere, now presented. And whilst, in contemplating it, we have doubtless been sending up to heaven our fervent aspirations that it might again be realised in us.

The means by which it had been achieved then, he claimed, was by the ministry of 'laborious, faithful, spiritual men of high attainments in personal religion' and it was to ensure such a ministry for their church in the nineteenth century that he proposed, at the 1828 synod, the establishment of a theological examination committee to test future candidates for ordination on their doctrinal orthodoxy and personal spirituality.

Looking back on the great revival of religion which came in 1859, the Rev William Richey of Coleraine observed:

> A great and blessed change ... had, for more than a quarter of a century before the Ulster awakening, been gradually taking place. There was far more earnestness in the use of the stated and ordinary 'means of grace'. The pulpit had been gaining both in pathos and power. Appeals to the conscience were more frequent and pointed. There was a fuller exhibition of the sovereignty of God, of the person, offices and grace of Christ, of the work of the Holy Spirit ... There had been much and earnest prayer for an outpouring of the Spirit prior to the Awakening.

It was the men who entered the ministry after the establishment of the Synod's theological examination committee who were largely responsible for this change.

Interest in, and prayer for, revival were stimulated by reports of a revival in America, which had begun in New York in 1857 and was spreading widely with large numbers experiencing conversion. The General Assembly of 1858, meeting in Londonderry, gave time to discussion of, and prayer for, revival and agreed to send two of its senior members to America to study and bring back information about what was happening. The Assembly also heard from the Rev John Moore of Connor in county Antrim about the growing number of conversions which were taking place within the bounds of his congregation, where prayer and cottage meetings were multiplying.

Later that year what was happening in Connor began to have repercussions in neighbouring districts and particularly in Ahoghill, where, according to the minister of the First

Presbyterian congregation, the Rev David Adams, conversions had also been taking place both in his congregation and in the former Secession congregation, Trinity, whose minister was the Rev Frederick Buick. J. H. Moore of Connor, Buick and Adams were all earnest evangelicals, and Adams claimed that revival had been a recurring theme of his preaching.

Communion seasons have been occasions of revival experience in Scottish Presbyterian history and figured prominently in Ulster's Six Mile Water Revival. A Monday evening service of thanksgiving for the previous day's communion in First Ahoghill church on 14 March 1859 became the occasion of the beginning of the Ulster Revival as a mass movement. According to 'Spectator', writing in the *Ballymena Observer*, a local newspaper, 'an impulse to address the audience fell suddenly, and apparently with all the power of prophetic inspiration, upon one of the "converted" brethren.' He insisted that 'he spoke by command of a power superior to any minister' and defied attempts to silence him. Fearing the collapse of the galleries in the overcrowded church, the minister, David Adams, disturbed by this challenge to his authority, cleared the building. Freed from ministerial disapproval, the speaker, one James Bankhead, addressed a crowd of some 3,000 people in the Diamond in the centre of Ahoghill and, according to 'Spectator':

> Amid the chilling rain and on streets covered with mud, fresh 'converts', moved by the fervency and apostolic language of the speaker, fell upon their knees in an attitude of prayer, a spark of electricity appeared to have animated and impressed a large number of the audience and it is confidently afforded that some, who went there to mock, were heard to pray.

A. R. Scott, in his doctoral thesis on the Revival, judged that:

> it would appear that, while a great work of grace smouldered in the Connor and Kells district, as it was also doing in Belfast, Comber, Antrim, Killyleagh, Bovea, Banbridge, Lurgan and Ahoghill, the flames burst forth in Ahoghill on the evening of 14 March 1859 and, from then onwards, things moved in an extraordinary manner.

The revival spread rapidly through much of Ulster and there were repercussions in the south of Ireland. There were gatherings of thousands of people in fair hills and market places. It was estimated that more than 35,000 attended a meeting in Belfast's Botanic Gardens on 29 June, to pray for and hear about the progress of the revival. As originally in Ahoghill there were dramatic scenes in many places, men and women falling down and crying out under conviction of sin. Such psychosomatic symptoms and other disturbing features – newly converted girls and boys claiming, as Bankhead had done in Ahoghill, direct divine authority for their utterances, reports of visions and miracles which caused critics of the revival like the Rev Isaac Nelson to claim in his *Year of Delusion* that superstition was triumphing and infidelity would result. Most Presbyterians, however, seem to have believed that 1859 was *The Year of Grace*, the title of Professor William Gibson's favourable account. They believed that the positive results of the revival in increased numbers of church members and their greater commitment to the life and work of the church, the wave of candidates for ordination and the new warmth and joy many experienced in Christian service, compelled them to regard the revival as 'an extraordinary dispensation of Providence'.

Others, like Isaac Nelson, have viewed the results of 1859 with a colder eye. David Hempton and Myrtle Hill, in their recent study of evangelical Protestantism in Ulster society, conclude that:

> Numerically, the claims of the revival's supporters are difficult to substantiate. While huge open-air meetings focused attention upon the popular response and some commentators considered 100,000 to be an underestimation of the number of converts, church statistics suggest that the sudden rise in membership figures was transient and probably most effective within the church's existing constituency.

They suggest that the major beneficiaries of the revival were the Baptists and Brethren 'for whom the period of the revival was particularly fruitful'. R. Coad, in his history of the Brethren movement, which had emerged in Dublin and Wicklow as a product of evangelicalism in the Church of Ireland, claims that the 1859 revival 'marked the beginning of the main growth of independent Brethren churches' in the north of Ireland. He recounts how Jeremiah Meneeley, a Presbyterian prominently involved in the origins of the revival in county Antrim, and the Rev J. E. McVicar, a Reformed Presbyterian minister, became Brethren evangelists.

The question of infant baptism, or, more properly, the baptism of the children of believers, was raised in the context of the revival as a result of the challenge of the Baptists and Brethren who practised believers' baptism. Another aspect of this question was the validity of the baptism of Roman Catholics who as revival converts became Presbyterians. Were they to be rebaptised? The General Assembly, following the lead of such impeccable Protestants as Henry Cooke, maintained the traditional Reformed view of the Roman Catholic Church as a part of the Visible Church, though, like all churches, in need of reformation under the word of God. Thus Roman Catholics who became Presbyterians in 1859 were not re-baptised, just as William Crotty, the former priest who had led members of his flock into the Presbyterian Church in Birr in 1839 had not been re-ordained.

Gibson claimed that the revival diminished sectarian tension in Ulster but Hempton and Hill insist that 'other sources tell a different story':

During the seventeenth century predestinarian theology had facilitated the Protestant community's perception of itself as 'God's people in Ireland surrounded on all sides by anti-Christian idolatry and superstition.' The rigidity of that doctrine was now in decline but the interpretation of the revival as a divine visitation – which had little or no impact on Roman Catholic areas – provided a nineteenth-century alternative. The revival movement offered reaffirmation, justification and divine approval to a society which had undergone half a century of social political and religious upheaval.

Thus the revival was 'another landmark in the religious dif-
ferentiation between Protestants and Catholics', which had become sharper as a result of the Protestant crusade.

The revival's emphasis on personal assurance of salvation
also raised questions about the way in which Presbyterians understood the Westminster Confession's teaching on election and
predestination. J. E. Davey, in his centenary history of the
General Assembly, reported that the revival 'brought a quite
new sense of assurance and of joy in Christian living'. 'Hitherto',
he claimed,

> a fairly rigid Calvinism had very generally been held, and
> the seeming arbitrariness or inscrutability of God's will
> therein depicted, gave little certainty of assurance – one
> could not be certain whether one was among the elect or not.
> Now faith was reinforced by feeling, by a consciousness of
> surrender and a joy in God and a note of certainty entered the
> life of the church, along with a new sense of evangelical re-
> sponsibility.

But not all Presbyterians welcomed these developments. The
nineteenth-century Presbyterian historian, W. T. Latimer, considered that ministers, as well as evangelists, became increasingly
emotional in their presentation of the gospel after 1859.
Traditionally they had aimed at 'bringing sinners to Christ, and
building up believers in holiness, by instructing the understanding rather than by exciting the emotions'. After the revival, in
Latimer's view, they began to appeal 'more to feelings rather
than to the intellect' and tended to emphasise 'only a few theological principles' rather than declaring 'the whole counsel of
God'. After the revival, evangelicalism remained a strong force
in Ulster Presbyterianism, renewed by the campaign of the
American evangelists, Moody and Sankey, in the 1870s and
Torrey and Alexander at the beginning of the twentieth century
and also by the evangelicalism, in rural areas, of bodies like the
Faith Mission, introduced from Scotland in 1890.

Revivalism has often been charged with anti-intellectualism
by distinguished American historians of ideas like Perry Miller

and church historians like John Kent. Others, like George Marsden and Mark Noll, have rejected such simplistic dismissals. Marsden has claimed that evangelicalism has had 'its own vigorous intellectual life', particularly when associated with Calvinism as in the person of Jonathan Edwards, in the Great Awakening in America in the eighteenth century. Evangelical professors of theology in Irish Presbyterianism like Robert Watts, who supported the visits of Moody and Sankey, and Richard Smyth who was involved in the 1859 revival, could scarcely be charged with anti-intellectualism. The fact that Irish Presbyterians built two theological colleges in the 1850s suggests that they has not abandoned their traditional intellectual understanding and presentation of the Christian faith.

The Presbyterian Synod's uneasy relationship with the Belfast Institution ended finally in 1840 when the divinity professors of the Non-subscribers were admitted to the college faculty on the same terms as the Synod's professors, who refused to co-operate with them in college acts of worship. In 1841 the General Assembly decided that the time had come when their church must have a college 'over which she shall have adequate authority and control'. The church moved slowly, however, for there was a genuine reluctance to end their relationship with the Institution and it was not until 1844 that a special meeting of the Assembly appointed a committee 'to take such steps as to them may appear expedient for the erection and endowment of a college for this Assembly'.

The situation was complicated, however, by a government announcement of its intention to establish new institutions of higher education in Ireland. This meant that any hope entertained by Presbyterians of government financial support for a Presbyterian college was extinguished. The government planned to found a new Irish university with three colleges, one in the north, one in the south and one in the west. After negotiations with the government, Henry Cooke and other members of the Assembly's college committee agreed to abandon the Assembly's planned college of arts and divinity, to recognise the new government college for the pre-theological education of their ministers, and accept government finance for seven professorships of theology and kindred subjects in a Presbyterian Theological College.

This did not satisfy some members of the college committee who refused to abandon the idea of a college of arts and divinity, claiming that the church would have no more – perhaps even less – influence and control over the proposed government college than it had had over the Belfast Institution, that 'nothing short of a complete Presbyterian college in arts and theology would meet the church's needs'. They were unable, however, to persuade a majority in the Assembly to share their view and the project of a Presbyterian college of arts and divinity might have been totally impracticable had it not received a benefaction of £20,000 from the estate of a Presbyterian minister's widow, Martha Maria Magee. The Assembly tried unsuccessfully to have Mrs Magee's bequest used to provide buildings for their theological college in Belfast but the court of chancery decided that it could only be used for a college of arts and divinity. Eventually Mrs Magee's trustees, with financial help from the citizens of Londonderry, who had been disappointed when the northern 'Queen's' College was sited in Belfast, and from the Honourable the Irish Society, major landowners in the northwest, build the Magee College in Londonderry as a college of arts and divinity. Meanwhile the General Assembly had built and opened a theological college, the Presbyterian College, popularly known as the Assembly's College, in Belfast in close proximity to the new government Queen's College. Having had no college of their own in which to train their ministers for the first two hundred years of their history, Irish Presbyterians now had two.

Irish Presbyterians did not only build two colleges in the nineteenth century. Writing in 1884 Thomas Croskery (a professor in Magee College) claimed that 'nearly one half of all our churches have been built or rebuilt and enlarged' since the formation of the General Assembly in 1840, and that 'nearly all our

391 manses' had been erected during the previous 25 years, many of them as a result of a church and manse fund, inaugurated in 1853. Unfortunately, in the second half of the century the simple classical style exemplified in May Street Church in Belfast, built for Henry Cooke in 1829, was superseded by more ornamental neo-gothic fashions, with soaring spies and grinning gargoyles. The climax of the nineteenth-century building boom came at the end of the century with the erection of a massive Church House and Assembly Hall in the centre of Belfast.

The Industrial Revolution in the Lagan valley, with the population of Belfast exploding from 20,000 in 1800 to 350,000 in 1901, posed enormous problems for a church whose structures had emerged gradually to meet the needs of pre-industrial society, which was largely rural. New congregations had to be gathered, church buildings provided and large scale outreach undertake. We have seen that evangelism was regarded as the church's proper response to the problem of industrial workers who saw the church primarily as a provider of rites of passage – christenings, marriages and funerals. Dedicated ministerial evangelists like Hugh Hanna, Tommy Toye and William Johnston were in the vanguard of the church's outreach to the new population of Belfast. In 1881 the Belfast Presbytery appointed a church extension committee with Johnson as its convener and in the next decade they succeeded in forming seven new congregations. Even this was probably too little too late and in the last ten years of the century the population of Belfast leapt from 250,000 to 350,000.

Irish Presbyterians, like other Christians, could not ignore the urgent social problems which accompanied the industrial revolution. Traditionally Presbyterians grappled with social problems at local or congregational level and in the early nineteenth century, in industrial Glasgow, Thomas Chalmers was still contending that the local parish and congregation could provide the best kind of caring community in which these problems could be solved. Others argued that they were too complex to be solved at parish or congregational level and in time Irish

Presbyterians, like others, were driven to develop new agencies to meet growing social challenges. The Kinghan Mission to the deaf and dumb (1857), the Sabbath School Society for Ireland (1862) and the Presbyterian Orphan Society (1866) were examples of these new agencies.

Intemperance or alcohol abuse was widespread in Ireland in all strata of society but particularly among the urban poor. Alcohol provided a fatal escape from the soul-destroying drudgery of industrial employment. It was John Edgar who launched the temperance crusade within Irish Presbyterianism. Temperance societies were formed and multiplied rapidly. Temperance soon became total abstinence in spite of Edgar's disapproval; he had opposed only excessive drinking and the use of spirits in particular. Gradually the habits of many Presbyterians changed; alcohol disappeared from such occasions as receptions following ordinations and installations and by the end of the century most ministers were total abstainers.

Worship in Reformed or Presbyterian churches has traditionally been plain and simple, characterised by the reading and preaching of the Word of God in Scripture, by the usually extemporaneous prayer of the presiding minister and the singing of metrical psalms as praise. The Synod of Ulster had allowed Scripture paraphrases to be sung in addition to psalms but this practice was dropped in 1840 in deference to the principles of the Seceders, who used only psalms in worship. The 1859 revival made hymn singing popular and in the later decades of the nineteenth century Irish Presbyterians were deeply divided over the question of hymn singing and the use of instrumental music in public worship. Popular practice prevailed eventually, in spite of persistent General Assembly prohibitions of the use of instrumental music – the Assembly never gave official recognition to the use of instruments – and organs and hymn singing were introduced gradually in Presbyterian churches. The first official hymnal was The *Church Hymnary*, which was published in 1898 in co-operation with the Church of Scotland and other Scottish Presbyterian churches though, a century later, the

Reformed Presbyterians or Covenanters still worship without the use of hymns or instrumental music.

Irish Presbyterians had links with Reformed and Presbyterian churches, not only in Scotland, but in Europe, the United States and in British colonies, in particular Canada, South Africa and New Zealand. In 1873 the General Assembly appointed a committee 'to correspond with other Presbyterian churches with the view of bringing about an ecumenical Council of such churches, to consider subjects of common interest to all, and especially to promote harmony of action in the mission fields at home and abroad.' The correspondence, taken up by other Presbyterian churches, led to the formation in 1875 of the World Presbyterian Alliance, forerunner of today's World Alliance of Reformed Churches which, in 1993, comprised 175 churches in more than 18 countries, and some 70,000,000 souls.

In politics most Presbyterians remained liberals for most of the nineteenth century. Probably the biggest political questions of the second half of the century were land ownership and Home Rule. Many Presbyterians were tenant farmers who resented the economic and political power of their landlords, most of whom belonged to the established Church. Presbyterian tenant farmers and their ministers were enthusiastic leaders and supporters of a campaign to achieve what became known as tenant right, its aims summarised by a Presbyterian minister, the Rev N. M. Brown of Drumachose in county Derry, as the three F's – fair rents, fixed tenure (no arbitrary evictions) and free sale of the tenant's interest in his holding. Landlord and government resistance aroused emotions and in the excitement of tenant-right meetings wild words were spoken. At Rathfriland in county Down in January 1850 the Rev John Rutherford identified landlords with the exploitation of their tenants and asked: 'Would they longer submit or would they rise in their might and demand their rights?'

Violent rhetoric of this kind and the fact that Catholic priests and Presbyterian ministers were sharing tenant-right platforms alarmed establishment Protestants like Henry Cooke who ac-

cused the tenant-right movement of communism and warned of
the folly of repeating the disaster of 1798. The General Assembly,
however, gave the movement its countenance, causing one of
the tenant-right leaders, the Presbyterian journalist, James
McKnight, to rejoice that,

> Our church is now in her natural position, namely, in that of
> a guardian and a witness on behalf of the poor man's rights,
> in opposition to the rich man's tyranny ... We can conceive of
> no alliance more unnatural or more degrading than that
> which has sometimes been brought into forced operation, be-
> tween our free Presbyterianism and the spirit of reactionary
> toryism.

The union of Presbyterian and Catholic in the tenant-right
movement was endangered by sectarian feeling when the
British government responded to the re-introduction of a
Roman Catholic hierarchy in Britain – hitherto a missionary
province governed by vicars apostolic – by passing an
Ecclesiastical Titles Bill which forbade Roman Catholic bishops
to take the titles of existing Anglican bishoprics. Catholics, particularly in Ireland, interpreted this as a new form of penal legislation and a Catholic Defence Association was formed in Dublin
in which Catholic tenant-right leaders were involved. In Britain
and Ulster an upsurge of anti-Catholic feeling followed the introduction of the English hierarchy. Henry Cooke, and even
Henry Montgomery, were among Presbyterian orators who addressed large gatherings in Belfast to protest against what Lord
John Russell, the British Prime Minister, had called 'this Catholic
aggression'. The tenant-right movement survived these sectarian
stresses, however, and its aims were achieved through government legislation, beginning with Gladstone's Land Act of 1870.

Before that Act was on the statute book, Gladstone had dis-
established the Church of Ireland, the landlords' church. There
had long been a question mark over the Church of Ireland, as the
church of a minority, being the national church. In 1867 the
Catholic hierarchy had declared that its continued existence as
the established Church was the fountainhead of 'the waters of

bitterness which poison the relations of life in Ireland and es-
trange from one another, Protestants and Catholics.' Few
Presbyterians followed Henry Cooke in his opposition to disestablishment even though disendowment, which followed disestablishment when the Roman Catholic hierarchy refused to
accept 'concurrent endowment', meant that *regium donum* payments for Presbyterian ministers ended. Existing beneficiaries
were to be compensated but the government agreed to add a
bonus payment if ministers handed over their compensation
payments to the church. Most ministers did and a fund was established from which Presbyterian ministers still benefit today.

So far most Irish Presbyterians supported Gladstone's re-
forming agenda in Ireland but they were horrified by his 'conversion' to Home Rule. As a liberal, Gladstone believed that
every nation had a right to self-government and that the least
Britain could offer Ireland was home rule within the British
state, the restoration of an Irish parliament. Most Irish
Protestants, however, believed that an Irish parliament would
mean Roman Catholic domination, that Home Rule would be
Rome Rule. Presbyterians, in particular, having suffered under a
Protestant ascendancy, were determined not to submit themselves to a Roman Catholic ascendancy.

The General Assembly agreed unanimously that:

a separate parliament for Ireland ... would, in our judgement
lead to the ascendancy of one class and creed in matters per-
taining to religion, education and civil administration. We do
not believe that any guarantees, moral or material, could be
devised which would safeguard the rights and privileges of
minorities scattered throughout Ireland against encroach-
ment of a majority vested with legislative and executive
functions.

At the same time the General Assembly made it quite clear
that Presbyterians were not opposed to change or reform.
Thomas Sinclair, then a leading elder in the church, who seconded
the Assembly's Home Rule resolution, emphasised that they
were not insensitive to the 'rights of the Irish people and the

wants of Ireland', for they, too, had suffered under religious dis-abilities but he, as a businessman, believed that Home Rule would be an economic disaster for Ulster which,

> would empty their mills, clear their rivers and shipyards, would stop their looms, would make the voice of their spin-dles silent and would cause a complete destruction of the in-dustry that had made the province so prosperous.

Perhaps there were many, even in Belfast, who had not shared in that prosperity and Sinclair was not to know that his malign scenario would become a reality under the Union a cent-ury later, but in 1886 it was a compelling argument for many Presbyterians as it had been in 1841 when used by Henry Cooke to oppose O'Connell's repeal movement.

Gladstone found it hard to understand that the Ulster Presbyterians who had led the United Irish movement a century before were implacable opponents of his Home Rule policy. An Ulster Presbyterian lawyer, J. J. Shaw, a former professor of logic and metaphysics in Magee College, offered an explanation in a pamphlet, *Mr Gladstone's Two Irish Policies, 1869 and 1886*. In op-posing Irish Home Rule, he argued they were not repudiating their United Irish ancestors:

> Catholic Emancipation, a reformed parliament, a responsible executive and equal laws for the whole Irish people. These were the real and declared objects of the United Irishmen. And it was only because they saw no hope of attaining these objects through an Irish parliament that they took up arms.

These objects of the United Irishmen had been achieved in the years since 1798 and were shared by all in Ireland as citizens of the United Kingdom, but would they be safe in an Ireland under a parliament dominated by one faction of the Irish people, a faction belonging to a church which taught that Protestants were heretics and that heretics had no rights? The nub of the Irish Presbyterian opposition to Home Rule was their lack of trust in an Irish Roman Catholic government to maintain civil and religious liberty for Protestants in Ireland.

By 1886 most Irish Presbyterians had abandoned one of the

objects of their United Irish ancestors, what William Drennan had defined as 'a total separation from Britain'. Their nineteenth-century experience had bound them economically, politically and spiritually to Britain, perceived as a great Protestant imperial power, called by God to civilise the world. The increasing identification of Irish Protestantism and unionism paralleled and was in part a consequence of the identification of Irish nationalism and the movement for Home Rule with the aspirations of Catholic Ireland. Shaw, like most of their spokesmen, insisted that they were Irish and loved Ireland, although they believed that the interests of all the people of Ireland were best secured by the union. They saw no contradiction in being both Irish and British.

Irish Presbyterian opponents of Home Rule resented allegations that they had all become Orangemen and tories. The Rev 'Roaring Hugh' Hanna, a vigorous and outspoken opponent of Home Rule and an Orangeman, declared that he knew of only three Orangemen among the ministers of the General Assembly. A Liberal Unionist Association was formed by men like Thomas Sinclair but as the Home Rule struggle intensified there was considerable pressure on opponents of Home Rule to unite under the umbrella of what became the Ulster Unionist party. The fact that the British Tory party espoused the unionist cause made it difficult for unionists to resist being drawn into the Tory camp.

The change in Presbyterian attitudes to Orangeism was reflected in the columns of the Presbyterian weekly newspaper, *The Witness*. In 1875 the annual Orange demonstrations had been reported without enthusiasm – 'Let us hope that the dead past will be allowed to bury its dead memories' – but in 1886 the Orange processions had become a 'magnificent display of loyal men prepared to defend the union at any sacrifice'. Already there were those who had begun to think in terms of armed resistance if Home Rule became a reality. A hundred years after their United Irish forefathers had taken up arms to achieve a separation from Britain, some Irish Presbyterians were contemplating taking up arms to preserve the union.

Other Presbyterians viewed all of this with strong disapproval. When Gladstone's second Home Rule Bill came before parliament in 1893 the unionist majority in the Irish General Assembly was challenged by a sturdy and articulate minority, led by men like the Rev J. B. Armour of Ballymoney who contended that Irish Presbyterianism had more to fear from unionism and the path unionists were following, than from Home Rule. Few gave them open support but when an anti-Home Rule resolution was carried in the 1893 General Assembly by 304 votes to 11 there were 341 abstentions.

The only issue rivalling Home Rule in the General Assembly's debates in this period was temperance. Irish Presbyterians had not only accepted 'temperance', understood as total abstinence, for themselves, they had mounted a crusade to outlaw the use of alcohol as far as possible in the whole community. One triumph was the Sunday Closing Act for Ireland in 1878, regarded as a monument to the brief political career of Magee professor, Richard Smyth, liberal MP for county Londonderry, 1874-78.

CHAPTER 5

The Twentieth Century: Changes and Challenges

The early years of the twentieth century in Ireland were overshadowed by the continuing Home Rule crisis. Although Gladstone's second Home Rule Bill of 1893 had passed the House of Commons it was rejected by the Lords. When the Parliament Act of 1911 removed the Lords' ultimate veto over legislation which had passed the Commons, it was clear that Asquith's Liberal government, dependent for its majority on Irish nationalist support, would bring in some measure of Home Rule for Ireland.

On the eve of the 1910 election which brought the Liberals to power, eleven former moderators of the Irish General Assembly took the unprecedented step of publishing a manifesto in which they contended that the interests of *all* the people of Ireland were best safeguarded by the union with Great Britain. Acknowledging that 'the grave errors of British rule in Ireland were written on the pages of history', they declared that 'the determination of the British people to provide just and equal legislation for this country had been clearly demonstrated but the establishment of an independent Irish parliament would reverse this process and set up a Roman Catholic ascendancy.'

In February 1912 a great convention of Presbyterians was held in the recently built Assembly Hall in Belfast. It was not an official court of the church, as the Rev J. B. Armour was quick to point out, though it was to be given a kind of retrospective recognition by the General Assembly in the following June, which escaped bitter division by accepting that Presbyterian reactions to Home Rule had been adequately expressed in the convention and so no fresh statement on the subject was necessary.

The climax of the Ulster Protestant campaign to resist Home

Rule was the signing of the Ulster Covenant on 28 September 1912. Its text, recalling the historic Scottish Covenants of the seventeenth century, was largely the work of the Presbyterian elder, Thomas Sinclair, and it pledged its signatories,

> humbly relying on the God whom our fathers confidently trusted … to stand by one another in defending for ourselves and for our children our cherished position of equal citizenship in the United Kingdom, and in using all means which may be found necessary to defeat the present conspiracy to set up a Home Rule parliament in Ireland.

The Moderator of the General Assembly, Dr Henry Montgomery, superintendent of the Shankill Road Mission in Belfast, was among 237,368 men who signed the Covenant with 234,046 women signing a parallel document. Undoubtedly resistance in arms was among 'all means which may be found necessary to defect the present conspiracy' and when an Ulster Volunteer Force was formed in 1913 the then Moderator of the General Assembly, the Rev James Bingham, described them as a 'great and noble army of men … preparing to defend themselves and us from the dangers that threaten our citizenship, liberties and religion … they had a right to resist and he was ready to share with them in their resistance.' *The Witness* began to carry reports of Volunteer parades, of sermons preached at parade services and of arrangements being made to provide hospitals and an indemnity fund to support the Volunteers if armed conflict became inescapable.

In the siege atmosphere which was developing, any opposition to the church's unionist majority could bring unpopularity and even hostility. Some ministers who opposed the campaign against Home Rule and their church's part in it found their position so uncomfortable that they went abroad to pursue their ministries elsewhere. A substantial minority remained, however, to persist in dissent, and although 'determined and unyielding opposition to Home Rule' was reaffirmed by the 1913 General Assembly by 921 votes to 43, there were 165 abstentions. There was no change in majority Assembly opinion in 1914, though church members were urged 'to promote peace and good order in the community', without any indication that this would not forbid armed resistance to Home Rule.

Asquith's Home Rule Bill became law in August 1914 but the fact that it was suspended because of the outbreak in the same month of the First World War prevented armed conflict in Ireland. Presbyterians and Catholics, unionists and Irish nationalists fought together for Britain and her allies in France but the war failed to bring the two sides of the Irish quarrel together. The Ulster Volunteer Force was largely recruited into the British army as the Ulster Division and suffered appalling casualties on the Somme in 1916. At Easter in the same year Irish republicans had rebelled in Dublin with German help, which confirmed unionist suspicions that Irish nationalists were essentially anti-British. An Irish Convention in Dublin in 1917 revealed the impossibility of reconciling the outlooks of the majorities north and south. The General Assembly declared that 'under no circumstances will we consent to come under the rule of a Dublin parliament'. The situation was exacerbated by the victory of the hard-line republican party, Sinn Féin, in the 1918 election, who followed their election success by establishing Dáil Éireann as an Irish parliament in defiance of Britain and declaring an independent Irish Republic. At the same time their military wing, the Irish Republican Army, began a campaign of guerrilla warfare to force Britain to withdraw from Ireland.

A partitionist solution to the Irish problem had begun to be canvassed even before the war but did not appeal to either unionists or nationalists. It was still being described as 'distasteful' by the Moderator of the General Assembly in 1920 but when the Government of Ireland Act of that year provided for two parliaments in Ireland, north and south, and a Council of Ireland to foster Irish unity, Presbyterians accepted reluctantly for the sake of peace. A parliament for Northern Ireland, embracing the six counties of Antrim, Down, Armagh, Tyrone, Fermanagh and Londonderry, was inaugurated by King George V in June 1921 and met in the Presbyterian College, Belfast until the parliamentary buildings at Stormont were completed in 1932. The first prime minister of Northern Ireland was a Presbyterian, Sir James Craig.

A month later a truce was agreed between the IRA and the forces of the Crown preparing the way for the Anglo-Irish treaty of 1921 which brought into existence the Irish Free State with dominion status similar to that enjoyed by Canada in the British Empire. Northern Ireland was given the right to opt out of the new Irish state which it exercised immediately. All of this fell far short of the full independence which Dáil Éireann had claimed for the whole of Ireland and was rejected by implacable republicans like Eamon de Valera who resumed the armed struggle against their former comrades who were now the army of the Irish Free State and who forced the 'rebels' to lay down their arms in May 1923.

The violence of the 1919-23 period, during the 'war of independence' and the ensuing civil war, brought great suffering to the Irish people and, in particular, to the minority population, north and south. The popular identification of Protestantism with unionism and Catholicism with nationalism exposed Protestants in the south and Catholics in the north to the violence of extremists. Not surprisingly, their sufferings were soon being interpreted by their co-religionists as evidence of religious persecution.

The reports of the State of the Country Committee to the General Assembly contained allegations that a campaign of extermination was being pursued in the south. In 1922 the Assembly was told that 'many members of our church have been shot or intimidated or deprived of their property and compelled to leave the country.' At the same time southern Presbyterian ministers stated in debate in the Assembly that they did not believe that any of their people were being attacked because of their religion. Most southern Presbyterians, like their brethren in the north, had unionist sympathies. They tended to regard the IRA as 'murder gangs' while republicans saw *them* as collaborationists, particularly during the war of independence.

Returning ex-servicemen in 1919 were suspected of continuing British associations and therefore 'legitimate' targets for attack.

Between 1915 and 1922 there was a sharp fall in the number of Presbyterians in southern presbyteries, in some cases, as in Cork and Munster presbyteries, of almost 50%. These losses must be seen against a background of falling population numbers going back to the nineteenth century. In a recently published autobiography, nonagenarian Laura Wood relates how the sturdy Presbyterian community and congregation in Ballinasloe where she grew up, melted away. Many young men had been killed in the war and afterwards many land agents and stewards, invariably of Scottish origin, and other management staff employed in the various large houses in the area, left and their houses were destroyed. Her father's shop was raided and their home 'burned to the ground' and eventually he and her mother moved to Belfast to which she had already gone as a student.

The Roman Catholic nationalist minority in Northern Ireland felt equally uncomfortable in their new situation under partition. When partition had been proposed as a possible solution to the problem of divided Ireland, Cardinal Logue and the northern bishops had voiced their determined opposition. If Protestants dreaded becoming a minority in Ireland under a Roman Catholic government, Roman Catholics in the north reacted to partition with 'shock, incredulity and resentment', to quote a Catholic historian. They had been cut off from the Irish nation as it was entering its promised land. Many were not prepared to recognise the legitimacy of Northern Ireland and adopted a policy of non-co-operation, while the IRA continued the war of independence in the north.

Belfast, with its long history of sectarian conflict, became a vicious battleground. In the worst period of violence, from 6 December 1921 to 31 May 1922, 89 Protestants, including members of the security forces, and 147 Roman Catholics were killed and many were wounded. Roman Catholic workers in the shipyards were brutally assaulted and driven from their jobs. There were shameful atrocities on both sides.

The ultimate restoration of peace in both parts of Ireland provided an opportunity for new beginnings and both governments expressed benevolent intentions towards their minority
populations. Whatever suspicions Presbyterians had about the
Irish Free State they gave it recognition as a legitimate state
whose government was entitled to the obedience of its citizens.
The General Assembly encouraged Presbyterians in the south
'to co-operate whole-heartedly with their Roman Catholic fel-
low-countrymen in the best interests of their beloved land.' In
1924 the Rev A. W. Neill, moderator of the Synod of Dublin, appealed to Presbyterians in the Free State:

> instead of wasting energy in regrets ... we must concentrate
> upon the business of building up our country's fortunes on
> sound lines ... we must give our best in honesty, sincerity,
> yes, and in love. That is where our religion meets its supreme
> test and exercises its highest functions.

Presbyterians were, of course, an insignificant and diminish-
ing minority in the Irish Free State. They had little choice but to
make the best of it. The situation in Northern Ireland was quite
different. There the Catholic and nationalist minority was significant – about one third of the total population – and they were
not without hope that their situation might change. It was believed that a Commission set up under the 1921 Anglo-Irish
treaty to determine the boundaries of Northern Ireland would
transfer large areas, including the city of Derry, to the Free State,
and Northern Ireland would cease to be a viable state. Northern
nationalists, including bishops, served on an Irish Free State
committee set up to explore ways of making it impossible for
Northern Ireland to survive.

What was needed, it has been suggested by an historian of
Ulster Unionism, P. J. Buckland, was a 'substantial and imagina-
tive attempt to win over the minority and to assuage their suspicions and fears'. And he continued, 'whether or not such an effort
would have succeeded it is impossible to say, but what is certain
is that no attempt was made, instead, policies were adopted
which confirmed and even heightened nationalist and Catholic

hostility'. What was created in Northern Ireland has been de-scribed by a British civil servant who worked in the province for twenty years, Sir Wilfrid Spender, as 'a factory of grievances', though he added that Northern Ireland had a strong competitor in that field in the Irish Free State.

The abolition of proportional representation for elections in Northern Ireland, both local and parliamentary, and the redraw-ing of constituency and ward boundaries were perceived by the nationalist minority as benefiting the unionist majority. Educ-ation proved to be another area of dissatisfaction. The refusal of Roman Catholics to participate in a committee set up by the Northern Ireland government to advise on the establishment of an education system weakened any influence they might have had. In the event, Lord Londonderry, Northern Ireland's first Minister of Education, introduced a secular system on principles not unlike the National Education System of 1831, but neither Protestant or Roman Catholic churchmen were willing to accept a system which forbade religious instruction during normal school hours.

Roman Catholics refused to participate in the state system and took responsibility for their own schools at great expense to the Catholic community. Protestants, on the other hand, with the support of the Orange Order, brought pressure to bear on the Northern Ireland Prime Minister, Sir James Craig to have changes made in the state system to enable them to accept it. While denominational teaching continued to be forbidden, non-denominational Bible instruction was allowed. This was unac-ceptable to the Catholic hierarchy, the Bishop of Down and Connor, Daniel Mageean, declaring that 'simple Bible teaching is based on the fundamental principle of Protestantism, the in-terpretation of sacred scripture by private judgement'. It has been suggested that the hierarchy might have been able to have regulations modified to accommodate their principles but they did not do so and the perception that the Northern Ireland gov-ernment had endorsed a Protestant state education system re-mained as a prominent grievance of the minority until a rapprochement between church and state enabled them to receive support from public funds.

A. T. Q. Stewart in his book *The Narrow Ground* has observed perceptively how, in Irish Presbyterian history, there has been 'an almost Manichaean duality of outlook, Old Light and New Light, fundamentalist and intellectual, extremist and moderate'. He has also discerned in 'the alternation between Old Light and New Light theology ... an even older pulse in the Presbyterian mind, that of revival and religious torpor'. In the 1920s Irish Presbyterianism experienced once more the excitement of evangelical revival and the bitterness of theological controversy.

There had been stirrings of revival in the early years of the century, in Tobermore in county Derry and around Ballymena in country Antrim, but the revivals had been local and temporary. In the early 1920s the General Assembly's State of Religion Committee reported an increase in the number of congregational missions and a rise in the numbers of new communicants – 6,360 in 1923. A controversial evangelist, the Rev W. P. Nicholson, began to make an impact, particularly in reaching many who were largely beyond the normal ministrations of the church, with his down to earth presentation of the gospel. His evangelistic missions, in Belfast and in large towns like Ballymena and Portadown, attracted overflowing congregations and there were many conversions.

Nicholson, though an Ulsterman, had been ordained in the United States, where he had been deeply influenced by American fundamentalism and its campaign against theological liberalism which, in the Irish Presbyterian context, might be described as New Light. Old Light may have been successful in banishing New Light in nineteenth-century Irish Presbyterianism but, in the twentieth century, New Light was shining brightly in the academic world of European and American Protestantism. Traditional views of the Scriptures and of their literary history were being challenged and classical Christian doctrines were being questioned. Old Light conservatives saw this as a process of apostasy, and fought back. A respected Irish Presbyterian minister, the Rev James Hunter of Knock in Belfast, took a lead in attacking what he saw as the insidious advance of error. Nicholson gave popular expression to these concerns and a Presbyterian Bible Standards League was formed and echoes of the campaign against the Belfast Institution a century before were audible in the condemnation of the Presbyterian College, Belfast, as 'a seed-bed of rationalism'.

The climax of this campaign came in 1926 in the trial before the General Assembly on a charge of heresy of the Rev Professor J. E. Davey. Davey, a professor in the Presbyterian College, was a brilliant scholar, a former Fellow of King's College, Cambridge, but the theological liberalism he articulated in his lectures and in his publications was alleged to be heretical. The title of one of his books, *The Changing Vesture of the Faith*, indicated the direction of his thinking, but to his critics it was the substance, and not merely the vesture of the faith, which he was changing. His defence of his position in the General Assembly won him an overwhelming verdict of acquittal. James Hunter and others of his accusers felt obliged by conscience to secede from the Irish Presbyterian Church, to form the Irish Evangelical, later the Presbyterian Evangelical Church, which, though small, has maintained its witness to conservative Calvinism. A generation later, another Ulster evangelist, claiming to stand in the tradition of Nicholson, Ian Paisley, was to cite Davey's acquittal as one of the justifications for constituting a Free Presbyterian Church of Ulster. Five elders from the Irish Presbyterian Lissara congregation were the originators of this Free Presbyterian Church, but Ian Paisley, who was to become the personification of Free Presbyterianism, was himself never a Presbyterian.

Within mainstream Irish Presbyterianism, Davey's acquittal was not intended to signal the church's abandonment of Christian orthodoxy – it was because the church was convinced of his essential orthodoxy that he had been acquitted – though another indication of advancing liberalism was the General Assembly's decision in 1928 to explain the terms on which subscription to the Westminster Confession of Faith by ministers and elders was to be understood as signifying 'a declaration of adherence' to 'the fundamental doctrines of the faith as set forth in the Westminster Confession', upon which the church claimed to be 'fully agreed', though the doctrines were not specified.

Another sign of change was a slow and tentative movement, against considerable resistance, to give greater order and coherence to public worship in Irish Presbyterianism. The Church of Scotland had pointed the way in a *Book of Common Order*, known as the *Euchulogion*, first published in 1867, with eleven editions following before 1924, drawing upon a wide range of Catholic liturgical tradition, east and west. Such developments were anathema to most Irish Presbyterians although occasional voices were raised in criticism of the alleged barrenness of much congregational worship. It was not until 1911 that the General Assembly was asked, the memorial coming from the Synod of Dublin, 'to prepare and issue a directory for public worship'. Without much enthusiasm the Assembly appointed a Dublin minister, the Rev J. C. Johnston of the Abbey congregation, to convene a committee to respond to the memorial. Johnston found himself facing what he called 'appalling' opposition, owing to Irish Presbyterians' 'hereditary hatred of anything in the form of a liturgy'. When the committee did produce a directory for public worship in 1923, its use was not authorised by the General Assembly. It was another twenty years before an official *Book of Public Worship* for use in the Presbyterian Church in Ireland was published. It was, of course, a guide, not a prescribed liturgy and no one was compelled to use it.

A second book appeared in 1965 drawing on the rich heritage of devotional literature of many churches and providing prayers and Scripture readings for the great festivals and seasons of the Christian year which are now widely observed in contemporary Irish Presbyterianism. In 1980 the General Assembly's Public Worship Committee was asked to prepare a series of experimental revisions of services and most of the material produced has been in contemporary language.

As Dr R. S. Tosh, author of a doctoral dissertation on the ori-

gins and development of Irish Presbyterian worship, has observed, 'Irish Presbyterian worship has been almost totally ver-
bal with the use of movement and gesture severely limited, usually confined to Sacramental actions and the laying on of hands.'
And he continued,

> Opinions will of course differ as to whether the absence of
> symbolism, colour and movement represents purity or im-
> poverishment, yet, in many congregations attempts to re-
> duce reliance on the spoken word alone are taking place, in
> the development of Family Services and the use of Christian
> drama.

The Charismatic movement and a widespread demand for
greater informality in worship are changing the face of Irish
Presbyterian worship today. The *Church Hymnary* of 1898 has
been revised twice and is in urgent need of further revision, and
is frequently supplemented if not displaced in public worship
by modern collections, like *Mission Praise* and *Glory to God*. Not
only organs but choirs, often robed, and musical groups lead
praise. Presbyterians of the past must be uncomfortable in their
graves.

Modernisation of worship is only one aspect of the Irish
Presbyterian Church's strategy of outreach in the community, to
make the Christian gospel attractive and relevant to the needs of
the age of the millennium. Demographic changes have continued to challenge church structures developed largely in a pre-industrial society. It has been estimated recently that one half of
the total membership of the Irish Presbyterian Church lives
within 15 miles of the centre of Belfast. This has evoked a massive programme of church extension. In the years between the
two world wars many new congregations which were to become large and vibrant were formed – Stormont and Cregagh
and Orangefield in east Belfast, Seaview and Glengormley in
north Belfast and McCracken Memorial in south Belfast, and
outside Belfast in Greenisland and Ballyholme. Six church buildings were destroyed during the air-raids of the Second World
War. Three were rebuilt, the others merging with neighbouring

congregations, with one, the old Third Belfast congregation in Rosemary Street uniting with Ekenhead congregation in north Belfast, to escape the decline which tended to afflict inner-city churches in post-war Britain and Ireland. The process of church extension has continued since 1945 with some 40 new congregations coming into existence, many of them in rapidly growing provincial towns like Antrim, Ballymena, Bangor, Coleraine, Larne, Lisburn, Newtownards and Portstewart.

New congregations have been formed, old congregations have declined. The Home Mission, which was originally responsible for church extension, has enabled small congregations in depopulated rural areas, particularly in the south and west of Ireland to survive and continue to bear their distinctive witness. Since partition numbers of Presbyterians have fallen in the south and west of Ireland, continuing a process which must be seen against a background of falling population figures and Irish Presbyterian population numbers in particular. An estimated 50,000 Presbyterians in southern Ireland at the time of partition has shrunk to some 15,000 today with the majority of these in Dublin and the three counties of the old province of Ulster which were excluded from Northern Ireland – Cavan, Monaghan and Donegal. Recent evidence suggests that this decline in numbers may now have been arrested and congregations in the Republic of Ireland are building new churches and church halls to accommodate growing numbers and expanding activities. They serve a community loyal both to the Presbyterian Church and to what most of them today regard with pride as their own nation and state.

There are more congregations in the Irish Presbyterian Church today than there were when the General Assembly was formed in 1840, but fewer church members. An estimated 650,000 church members in 1840 have been reduced by half in the intervening years. Although this fall may partly be explained by falling population numbers in Ireland, they are mainly attributable to emigration and the advance of secularism, accompanied by a growing popular disenchantment with institutional

Christianity. The Presbyterian Church has responded to these challenges by continuing to proclaim the Christian gospel and give pastoral care and training in Christian discipleship to its members. While the ordained ministry has remained central to the church's life, there has been an increasing emphasis on the ministry of church members. When the foundation of the New University of Ulster, now the University of Ulster, brought to an end the special relationship between the Presbyterian Church and Magee College in Derry, which was incorporated in the new university, provision was made in the Magee University College, Londonderry Act of 1970, for payments resulting from a sale of property and transfer of endowments to be used to establish a Trust Fund for the purposes of training and education in the Presbyterian Church. Some of the Fund's resources have been used to set up a Christian Training Centre, appropriately called Magee House, in Belfast. Under the leadership of its first Director, the Rev Harold Graham, it has provided a wide range of in-service courses for ministers and training courses for elders and church members in Magee House itself and in a wide variety of locations throughout the church.

The take-over of Magee University College also enabled the General Assembly to transfer Magee Theological College, originally the theological department of the Magee College of Arts and Divinity, to Belfast to unite with the Presbyterian College to form what is now Union Theological College, thus rationalising the nineteenth-century duplication of theological colleges in the Irish Presbyterian Church. The church continues to maintain the Reformed tradition of an educated ministry. Today there are more older candidates for ordination, coming from a variety of employment backgrounds and, since 1976, women have been ordained. All still are expected to be university graduates before beginning their theological studies. Union Theological College is closely associated with the Faculty of Theology, now the Institute of Theology, in Queen's University, Belfast, in which the Union professors are recognised university teachers working in co-operation with the staffs of other colleges in the

Institute – Edgehill Methodist College, the Irish Baptist College, the Belfast Bible College and St Mary's College. Most Union students take a university degree in theology and an interesting development of recent years is the increasing number of students studying theology without being ordinands. Overseas and postgraduate students complete the wider college community.

Christian education for all begins of course in the home and in the Sunday schools and Bible classes of congregations. Since 1863 the Sabbath School Society for Ireland has provided resources for Christian education in homes and Sunday schools – systems of lessons, teachers' guides and training courses for Sunday School teachers. Since 1905 its bookshop, now known as Family Books, has not only been a resource centre for Christian education in the church but has contributed significantly to the finances of the Sabbath School Society. The Rev Ian McKee, convener of the General Assembly's Church Education Committee and Sunday School organiser, travels throughout the church conducting training classes and conferences for Sunday School teachers. This committee investigates and keeps the wider church informed about contemporary thinking on the subject of Christian education and the place of the child in the church.

The General Assembly's state and university education committees likewise keep the church informed about education in the wider community, which has always been a subject of concern to Presbyterians. Representatives of the church remain involved in the management committees of state schools, formerly church schools, which have been transferred to the state system. Religious education in schools continues to be a concern of the Presbyterian Church which has co-operated with other churches in the provision of schemes of religious education for schools. Some Presbyterian ministers have become Religious Education teachers in schools, others, Religious Education advisers to Education and Library Boards. The great expansion of higher or tertiary education in the second half of the twentieth century has brought an enormous increase in the numbers both of institutions of higher education and of students going on to third-level education. Presbyterian chaplains have been appointed to these institutions north and south who work closely with the chaplains of other churches in their ministry to these academic communities.

Young people in general are, of course, a primary concern for any Christian church. There are youth organisations and clubs in most Irish Presbyterian congregations. In the first half of the present century, what were called Boys' and Girls' Auxiliaries played an important role in stimulating young people's interest and participation in the life and mission of the Presbyterian Church. What have been called the 'uniformed organisations' – the Boys' and Girls' Brigades, the Boy Scouts and Girl Guides provided their members with a wide range of creative and recreational activities and from their ranks have come many leaders, not only in the organisations themselves, but in the wider church and community. They do not appeal to all young people, however, and a wide range of youth clubs and fellowships have developed under the umbrella of the church. In 1966 the General Assembly appointed its first fulltime Youth Secretary and since then the church's staff responsible for youth work has grown. A Youth Office in Church House is a resource centre for this work under the General Assembly's Youth Board through which the church is made aware of the needs and problems of young people today.

In 1980 a programme of youth evangelism was launched, under the title Youthreach, culminating in a youth festival on the campus of the University of Ulster in Coleraine in 1981. After sixteen years this Youthreach Festival has been discontinued, perhaps temporarily, and has been replaced by two events, one focusing on Bible study for young people over 16, and another, more in the Youthreach tradition, for the 11-16 age group.

There are three residential Presbyterian youth centres, at Castlerock and Rostrevor in Northern Ireland and Lucan in the south. Greatly extended facilities in Lucan were officially opened on 20 April 1998 by the President of Ireland, Mrs Mary McAleese. Presbyterian Youth Development projects have been grant-aided by the Department of Education of the Republic of Ireland. Reconciliation in a divided society has figured prominently in the agenda of youth organisations which bring Presbyterians into association with young people of other churches. In 1997 a team of young Presbyterians visited South Africa in the first leg of an exchange visit in which they studied the whole process of reconciliation which has taken place in South Africa. This was only one of many groups of Irish Presbyterian young people who have visited such countries as Nepal and Hungary while others have given up their summer holidays to become involved in congregational outreach and social service in Ireland.

Summer outreach to holidaymakers north and south, particularly on caravan sites, using youth groups, is part of Presbyterian evangelism strategy today. Evangelism has necessarily remained a characteristic of Irish Presbyterian church life in the twentieth century. Congregational evangelistic missions have continued to be popular methods of outreach and church-wide simultaneous missions have been organised at roughly ten year intervals. In the 1960s a Christian Stewardship and Lay Evangelism movement called church members to renewed commitment to Christ and his church, stressing the importance of ordinary church members in outreach. This was also a feature of Flame '74, a three phase programme of evangelism, launched in 1974, and organised by a new Board of Christian Training and Evangelism, formed in 1966. In the first phase church members were challenged to commitment to Christian service, in the second they were given training for the third phase, which was directed towards outsiders. Also in 1974 the Irish Mission was brought under the umbrella of the Board of Christian Training and Evangelism and the Mission's superintendent was made secretary to the Board, and evangelism secretary of the General Assembly. The Irish Mission continues to fulfil its original aim of bringing the challenge of Christ and knowledge of his gospel to Irish people of every denomination without proselytism.

As the second Christian millennium draws towards a close, Irish Presbyterians have launched an ambitious evangelistic campaign, calling upon every congregation in the church to reach out with the good news of Jesus Christ in their own area in a way that is appropriate to their situation. Life 2, as the campaign is called, with overtones of another dimension to life, here and hereafter, was launched on 13 September 1998 and continued until June 1999.

Since 1840 Irish Presbyterian outreach has extended far beyond the shores of Ireland. In every generation some of Irish Presbyterianism's most gifted sons and daughters have followed in the footsteps of Hope Waddell, Thomas Leslie, James Glasgow, Alexander Kerr and their families, pioneers of Irish Presbyterian outreach in the wider world. They have gone to share their faith, to heal the sick and to educate. Churches, hospitals, schools and colleges are continuing monuments to their self-sacrificing service.

Today the Presbyterian Church in Ireland no longer thinks in terms of a 'foreign' mission but maintains its responsibility

to proclaim the gospel in word and action in such countries and in such ways as the General Assembly and its Overseas Board may from time to time determine, wherever possible with churches in that country or area.

The original spheres of Irish Presbyterian outreach overseas were India and China and they remain areas of special interest and links with their churches remain strong. Irish Presbyterians are also involved in the work of partner churches in Jamaica, Malawi, Kenya, Indonesia, Israel, Brazil and Nepal and relationships with churches in Pakistan, Thailand, Myanmar, Togo, Zambia and the Sudan have been developing. Links with churches overseas are now reciprocal with ministers from India, Africa and Jamaica being welcomed for periods of service in Ireland.

The old Colonial and Continental Missions and the Mission to Jews have been replaced by committees of the Overseas Board with responsibility for relations with churches in the British Commonwealth, in Europe and in the Middle East. In recent years links with Reformed Churches in Europe, in France, Spain,

Italy, the Czech Republic, Hungary and Romania have been extended and strengthened.

Women, as missionaries and as wives of missionaries, have
played a prominent part in the Irish Presbyterian contribution to
Christian outreach in the world. In 1873 a 'Female Association
for promoting Christianity among the Women and Girls of the
East' was formed in Ireland and congregational auxiliaries
multiplied quickly. The following year Susan Brown, sister of a
missionary, was commissioned for service in India and in 1876
she founded a girls's high school at Surat. Almost a century
later, in 1967, Mena Williamson, its last Irish headmistress,
handed over a school of 424 girls to its first Indian principal,
Mabel Sacha. Susan Brown was the first of many Irish
Presbyterian women who have responded to Christ's call to
preach and teach and heal in his name in the wider world. In
1971 various women's organisations joined together to form the
Presbyterian Women's Association, popularly known as the
P.W.A., to unite and develop the Christian witness and service
of Irish Presbyterian women at home and abroad.

In 1909 an order of deaconesses was founded and today
some 27 deaconesses work in congregations, hospitals and community service under the Home Department of the P.W.A. They
are members of the worldwide Order of Deaconesses and undergo training for their special ministry. They are admitted to
the courts of the church, kirk session, presbytery, Synod and
General Assembly from which women were excluded until the
present century. Since 1926 women have been ordained as elders
and since 1976 as ministers in the Presbyterian Church in Ireland,
the Rev Ruth Patterson, daughter of a former Moderator of the
General Assembly, the first woman minister to be ordained.

The Rev Ruth Patterson is currently the Director of Restoration
Ministries, an ecumenical renewal and counselling initiative
based in Belfast. Irish Presbyterians, men and women, have
found outlets for Christian witness and service in a variety of ecumenical and inter-denominational agencies, including the
Evangelical Alliance, Scripture Union, the Irish School of

Ecumenics and the Corrymeela Community of Reconciliation, founded by a Presbyterian minister, the Rev Ray Davey. Many have gone overseas in the service of inter-denominational missionary societies like the Overseas Missionary Fellowship (formerly the China Inland Mission, and the Wycliffe Bible Translators). One such society of special interest to Irish Presbyterians is the Qua Iboe Fellowship which began in the pioneering evangelism in Nigeria of an Irish Presbyterian, Samuel Bill. Bill went to Nigeria in 1887 and today there are more Christian congregations in existence as a result of the Fellowship's witness in Nigeria than there are in the Presbyterian Church in Ireland and over the years many Irish Presbyterians have been involved in its work.

Dr John Mackay, former President of Princeton Theological Seminary in New Jersey, in which many Irish Presbyterian ordinands have studied, has suggested that:

> The church does not fulfil its full mission in the world as an instrument of God's glory when it is merely concerned with preaching the Word, adminstering the sacraments, producing Christian piety and carrying on its own institutional life. It has also a mission to the community.

Irish Presbyterians, like all Christians, are called to promote God's justice and righteousness in community, as well as in personal life, to be a prophetic voice in contemporary society. In 1921, as Northern Ireland was taking shape, the General Assembly offered a 'Programme for Social Reform' which anticipated many of the features of the modern welfare state – maternity benefits and child welfare centres, raising the school-leaving age to 16, provision of facilities for juvenile recreation, arbitration procedures for industrial disputes, state sponsored employment schemes, reform of the Poor Law and the care of the handicapped. This was very much in line with the vision of society we find in Calvin's Geneva, characterised by a concern for children and the poor and the promotion of honesty and integrity in commercial life.

These notes have been struck again and again in Presbyterian deliverances on social questions. When their shared experience of deprivation united Protestant and Roman Catholic have-nots in protest and rioting in Belfast in 1932, an episode graphically recorded in Paddy Devlin's moving account, *Yes, We Have No Bananas*, the Presbytery of Belfast joined with other church bodies in protesting on behalf of the victims of inadequate unemployment benefit and the Northern Ireland government responded by ordering Belfast Board of Guardians to double the current rates of outdoor relief. The Second World War raised many questions about the kind of society which should emerge after the war and in 1944 the General Assembly declared that

> in all plans for the future, human values must be placed centrally, and that all social, financial and economic systems must serve the highest welfare of men and women so as to ensure the fullness of life which God requires.

It must be acknowledged that it is much easier to enunciate lofty principles and ideals than to campaign determinedly for their implementation, especially when powerful vested interests have to be challenged. The Irish Presbyterian Church has sometimes been frankly critical of its own short-comings. In 1976 the Assembly's doctrine committee confessed that the church had often 'failed to bear the cross, to serve human needs to pioneer and persist in the search for justice, peace and reconciliation', and it continued:

> The church has always been tempted to support or refrain from criticising those in power, if its own life is made easier by compliance, and it has often failed to protest against injustices, because its leaders and members are not directly affected themselves or even seem to benefit from these injustices.

A recent study of what has been called 'The Nonconformist Conscience' in Victorian Britain has shown that churchmen usually found it easier to act effectively on clear moral issues like sexual promiscuity, intemperance and gambling than on complex problems of social, economic and industrial relations, and this has been the experience of Irish Presbyterians.

At the same time, confronted by a wide range of human

need, they have not always 'passed by on the other side', like the priest and Levite in Jesus' story of the Good Samaritan. Irish Presbyterian social action in the second half of the twentieth century has been summarised as including,

the provision of various hostels and homes for young and old; assistance of the poor, the orphan and the aged; concern for the alcoholic and other addicts; a Christian ministry to the deaf and dumb, to those in prison, to those serving in the Forces.

The Presbyterian Orphan Society, now the Orphan and Children's Society, continues to serve the needs of deprived families and children. One of its provisions is a Child Contact Centre in Belfast which enables children to maintain contact with the absent parent in a broken marriage. The Kinghan Mission, now the Kinghan Church, continues to minister to the deaf and dumb. In 1944 a boy's residential club was opened in Belfast to serve the needs of boys serving apprenticeships, who had to live away from home, and boys who had been before the courts. Forced to close in 1974 it reopened a decade later in new premises appropriately named the W. J. Thompson Memorial House, the Rev W. J. Thompson having been the founder of the original boys' club.

In 1949 a Presbyterian Residential Trust was established to provide care for the elderly and in 1950 the first home for the elderly, Adelaide House, was opened in south Belfast. It has been followed by others in Dublin, Portrush, Newcastle, Bangor, Londonderry and in the Belfast area. The Trust is an example of the fruits of co-operation between church and state, as is the Presbyterian Housing Association which also receives financial help from government and statutory social services. Similarly state assistance has enabled the Shankill Road Mission to refurbish and expand its facilities which now include a hostel for single homeless. Presbyterian Church in Ireland, or P.C.I. Enterprises, provides training for long-term unemployed men and women using funds provided under a government Action for Community Employment programme. Carlisle House, at

Carlisle Circus in Belfast, is a residential centre for alcoholics and drug addicts seeking rehabilitation.

In Dublin the Scots' Centre, an administrative and resource centre for ventures in social service, has been opened with the aid of grants from the Republic of Ireland's Department of Social Welfare and the Presbyterian Association Foundation. Under its umbrella, there have been ventures in social service such as the Dolebusters' advice and recreation centre for the young unemployed, organised by the Adelaide Road congregation. Other Presbyterian congregations, north and south, have developed their own schemes of social service to their local community, and ministry to the unemployed.

Responding to the challenges of the rapidly changing modern world has forced the Irish Presbyterian Church to follow a process of centralisation which began in the nineteenth century and has accelerated since the second world war. When the General Assembly was formed in 1840 the church had no central bureaucracy – even the clerkship of the Assembly was held by a parish minister in addition to his congregational responsibilities. Today the complexity and volume of the work done by the central agencies of the church have meant that a staff of fulltime officials has become necessary, supported by a growing body of secretarial assistants. Church House, built in the centre of Belfast at the beginning of the twentieth century, accommodates this growing bureaucracy and the Hall in which the General Assembly meets. It has recently been refurbished to prepare for the challenges of the twenty-first century.

These developments have required substantial financial commitments and in the 1960s a central committee began to co-ordinate the financial needs of the different agencies and funds of the church and set targets before presbyteries and congregations. This led to the emergence of the United Appeal Board which oversees the finances of the agencies of the church, evaluating their claims for financial support, and determining the level of that support. It currently requires an annual income of £2,500,000 to meet their needs. The total budget of the church is much greater, however, somewhere in the region of £15,000,000.

Although more and more of the church's work is organised and directed by the boards, commissions and committees of the General Assembly, the Presbyterian structure of the church is maintained, major questions of policy or constitutional change being submitted to presbyteries – of which there are twenty-one – for comment and approval before final decisions are taken by the General Assembly. In addition, presbyteries are involved in the central decision-making process through their representatives on commissions, boards and committees.

On the political question which divided and still divides the people of Ireland, the majority of Presbyterians, resident in Northern Ireland, remain unionist in sympathy, though most of those who live in the Republic of Ireland have long since ceased to regard themselves as British, The experience of the years since partition has widened rather than narrowed this difference in political outlook, as Dennis Kennedy has shown in *The Widening Gulf: Northern Attitudes to the independent Irish State, 1919-49*. In 1940, in the context of the second world war, in which the Irish Free State remained neutral, J. E. Davey wrote in his centenary history of the General Assembly:

> Whatever quarrels with British policy members of the Assembly may have had from time to time, and whatever their views of the best solution of the Irish problem, the sentiment of loyalty towards and pride in the British inheritance and commonwealth of peoples has been common to us all.

Twenty years later, in his *Short History of the Presbyterian Church in Ireland*, J. M. Barkley quoted Davey's words which he described as 'very true'. The last thirty years may have brought increasing dissatisfaction with British policy in Northern Ireland but has not changed the general political outlook of the majority of Northern Ireland's Presbyterians. Like J. J. Shaw in 1886, they see no contradiction in being both Irish and British but they want to remain within the United Kingdom.

The fact that the Roman Catholic Church refused to recognise the Northern Ireland state at the time of partition and, as Mary Harris has documented in *The Catholic Church and the*

Establishment of Northern Ireland, campaigned actively to deni-
grate and destabilise it, did nothing to moderate the anti-
Catholicism of many Ulster Presbyterians. At the same time the
position and influence of the Roman Catholic Church in the
southern state seemed to confirm Presbyterian suspicions that
Home Rule would mean Rome Rule. Gradually and inevitably
the Catholic and Gaelic ethos of *Saorstat Éireann* took institutional
shape. Compulsory Irish in schools, a ban on the sale of contra-
ceptives, the closure of the narrow and expensive avenue to divorce which existed in law, a new constitution in 1937 which
gave official recognition to 'the special position of the Holy,
Catholic, Apostolic and Roman Church as the guardian of the
Faith professed by the great majority of the citizens' were clear
indications of the new situation.

Irish Presbyterians had no desire to mount a crusade in defence of contraception and divorce and the General Assembly
openly acknowledged, from time to time, the helpfulness of the
southern government, particularly on the issue of Protestant
education. Indeed Presbyterians in *Saorstat Éireann* found their
position in general comfortable enough so long as they lay low
and said nothing.

Northern Presbyterians felt under no compulsion to do likewise and were quick to represent pressures on their southern
brethren as persecution. They drew attention to incidents and
attitudes, decisions of the courts and the government as evidence that, in the words of an Irish Mission report in 1936, 'the
Roman Catholic Church was putting forth every effort to make
Ireland a wholly Roman Catholic country'. At the same time the
Presbyterian Prime Minister of Northern Ireland, Lord
Craigavon, was declaring in Stormont that 'we are a Protestant
parliament and we are a Protestant state'. In creating what was
in fact, if not in law, a Protestant state in the north and a Roman
Catholic state in the south, Irishmen had not only failed to bring
in a new era of peace following partition but had succeeded in
creating what have been two factories of grievances.

Roman Catholic spokesmen excelled their Presbyterian

counterparts in exposing and denouncing what they saw as the persecution of their people. In his Lenten pastoral in 1938, Dr Daniel Mageean, Bishop of Down and Connor, alleged that the history of the Northern Ireland parliament was 'one long record of partisan and bigoted discrimination in matters of representation, legislation and administration'. In 1941, during the second world war, Cardinal MacRory, who had earlier declared that the Protestant churches were 'not even a part of the Church of Christ', claimed that the greatest example of oppression and tyranny in the world was the Northern Ireland state.

Extravagant statements of that kind helped Presbyterians to dismiss Roman Catholic allegations of discrimination as partisan propaganda. Even J. E. Davey, the quintessential Irish Presbyterian liberal, judged that 'the Roman Catholic harbours a love of grievance which finds imaginary grounds where real ones do not exist and exaggerates them greatly when they do'. Davey, though active in promoting reconciliation and tolerance, shared deep-seated Presbyterian suspicions of Roman Catholicism. 'Intolerance is the only thing which cannot easily be tolerated', he wrote on one occasion:

This is particularly difficult for the Protestant, for if he is intolerant he is being false to his principles, and, regrettably there have been such cases. For a Roman Catholic, on the contrary, in a considerable measure, intolerance is an accepted principle.

Davey's view of Protestant tolerance clearly reflected his own liberal Protestant outlook.

Such a climate of opinion on both sides was hostile to progress in religious and political dialogue and mutual understanding. Nevertheless, by the 1950s there were some signs of a change in climate. In 1950 the General Assembly's committee on national and international problems, in a report on 'The duties of Christians in relation to political and religious differences in Ireland', acknowledged that, while Presbyterians often feared Roman Catholic policies in religion, politics and social issues, their Christian duty was 'to stand for the spirit of reconciliation

... against the spirit of suspicion and enmity'. A Christian's first loyalty must always be to Christ and 'his loyalty to any party or state must not be allowed to conflict with his higher allegiance.'

Irish Presbyterian concern for justice was not merely theoretical. In 1956 when the Northern Ireland government was considering proposals to limit family allowances to the first three children in the family, which would have discriminated against the normally larger Roman Catholic families, the General Assembly protested against the proposal and appointed a deputation to express their protest to the government at Stormont.

Change accelerated in the 1960s and this may have been one reason why a decade which began with such promise should have ended in confrontation and conflict. The pontificate of John XIII and the Second Vatican Council signalled a revolution in Roman Catholic attitudes and there was a reciprocal response from Irish Presbyterians. In 1961, Dr Austin Fulton, outgoing moderator of the General Assembly, urged Presbyterians to reach out to Catholics in Christian charity exploring ways of co-operation for the common good. Two years later the Assembly stood in tribute to Pope John, whose death was announced during the Assembly's opening meeting and only one voice was raised in protest on the following day.

The decree on ecumenism of Vatican II was welcomed by the General Assembly in 1965, and a resolution of penitence for past Presbyterian uncharitableness was carried. There were reciprocal gestures from the Roman Catholic side. In 1963 Michael Hurley, professor of Dogmatic Theology at Milltown Park in Dublin, a leader in fostering relations with the 'separated brethren', edited a handbook of meditations and prayers, entitled *Praying for Unity* to which the moderator of the General Assembly, Dr W. A. Montgomery, contributed, as did other Protestant church leaders. Conferences of Roman Catholics and Protestants began to meet at Glenstal Abbey near Limerick (1964) and Greenhills in Drogheda (1966) providing opportunities for dialogue.

In 1966 another report of the General Assembly's national

and international problems committee, on the controversial subject of religious discrimination in Ireland, acknowledged that it was a reality, explaining though not condoning it as a symptom of mistrust and suspicion. But not everyone in the Presbyterian community in Northern Ireland sympathised with these irenical developments. As often in Ireland religion and politics were intertwined and when Terence O'Neill, the Stormont Prime Minister attempted to build bridges between the two communities he was portrayed as a traitor to unionism and Irish Presbyterian 'ecumenists' were accused of leading a 'Romeward trend' in Irish Presbyterianism.

Political and theological conservatism found a voluble and effective spokesman and leader in Ian Paisley, the permanent moderator of the Free Presbyterian Church of Ulster. Since 1951 he had been leading a relentless campaign against mainstream Irish Presbyterianism; he combined this now with an equally vociferous campaign against mainstream unionism and the unionist Prime Minister, Terence O'Neill. He led dissident unionists in forming a Democratic Unionist Party as he had led dissident Presbyterians to form the Free Presbyterian Church of Ulster and both flourished in a climate of increasing religious and political tension. In 1966 the opening meeting of the General Assembly became the occasion of an intemperate protest led by Paisley, who was subsequently found guilty of unlawful assembly and sent to prison for three months when he refused to give an assurance to keep the peace, which he interpreted as an attempt to silence his denunciations of error. As Dennis Cooke has written in his portrait of Ian Paisley, *Persecuting Zeal*, 'clergy and politicians, he maintained, were conspiring to betray Ulster'.

Also in 1966, the temperature of sectarianism was raised by nationalist and republican celebrations of the fiftieth anniversary of the 1916 Easter Rising. In the same year the murder of a Catholic barman, Peter Ward, by a loyalist paramilitary organisation which had assumed the name Ulster Volunteer Force, in imitation of the Volunteer Force raised to resist Home Rule in 1912, was a dismal portent of the vicious spiral of violence which was to last thirty years at a cost of over 3,000 lives, many thousands more maimed and injured and large scale destruction of property.

It goes without saying that the Presbyterian Church has continuously condemned the violence of the past thirty years and from time to time the General Assembly has acknowledged, and expressed penitence for, the contribution of Presbyterians to division and conflict. Presbyterian ministers and church members have been active in situations of communal violence, endeavouring to reduce tensions and promote peace. At the same time there has been widespread dissatisfaction with some of the steps taken by the British government to solve what has become known as the Northern Ireland problem. When the Northern Ireland parliament was prorogued in 1972 the General Assembly deplored

the decision of the United Kingdom government to prorogue the Northern Ireland parliament and the consequent denial to the democratically elected representatives of the people a voice in the government of their country and we further deplore that this action taken now is above all else at the expense of a peaceful majority who have sought to maintain their cause in an orderly and lawful way.

At the same time Presbyterians were enjoined to 'keep as our first aim the peace and welfare of our land and the reconciliation of our divided country'.

Positive initiatives taken from time to time to try to restore devolved government to Northern Ireland have been welcomed and supported by the General Assembly. When a Northern Ireland Assembly was elected in 1973 the General Assembly urged members of the new Assembly to work together for the common good, and the Sunningdale Agreement of December 1973 which initiated a short-lived experiment in 'power-sharing' between representatives of Northern Ireland's two communities was welcomed by the General Assembly and its collapse in 1974 deplored.

A commitment to the continuing union between Great

Britain and Northern Ireland has remained the characteristic political outlook of a majority of Irish Presbyterians. When a New Ireland Forum was set up in 1983 as an Irish nationalist attempt to find a way forward in the Irish political situation indicating the possible shape of a future united Ireland state, the General Assembly decided not to submit evidence though the Synod of Dublin, located wholly in the Irish Republic, did. When the Forum's report was published the General Assembly expressed disappointment that, in its view, it did not provide 'an acceptable framework for the solution of our present problems', while the Assembly's Government committee criticised its failure to come to terms with the unionist viewpoint.

The subsequent Anglo-Irish Agreement which gave the Irish Republic a say in the affairs of Northern Ireland was condemned by the General Assembly as inevitably bringing 'great distress to many members of the majority population' in Northern Ireland. In successive years the General Assembly has continued to urge the British and Irish governments to re-examine the Agreement and finally in 1989, the Assembly, by 235 votes to 183, called upon the governments to 'cease to operate the Agreement which has so obviously failed to achieve peace, stability and the defeat of terrorism.' Significantly, however, the majority in favour of this call was not very large.

Irish Presbyterians have always declared their opposition to political violence from whatever quarter, with loyalist terrorists being condemned as vigorously as republican. Recent ceasefires have been welcomed as has what has become known as the Good Friday Agreement of 1998 providing for a new devolved power-sharing government for Northern Ireland. The General Assembly in June called for 'continued constructive leadership' which 'should be exercised in a spirit of generosity and goodwill, integrity and sensitivity, to ensure that the proposed arrangements succeed, for the well-being of everyone in both parts of the island.' The Assembly also reminded political parties that, having signed the Mitchell Principles – disavowing political violence – they were 'morally bound to actively support

the decomissioning of paramilitary weapons.' On the contentious issue of Orange parades, the Assembly urged the pur-
suit of local agreements but, where such agreement could not be
reached, those who parade and those who protest should 'abide
by lawfully taken "determinations" of the Parades Commission',
the body set up by government to adjudicate on 'contentious'
parades.

Closely related to political questions in Ireland has been the
question of inter-church relations, in particular, relations between Presbyterians and the Roman Catholic Church. The
twentieth century has witnessed a great movement towards
Christian unity, reversing the process of disunity of previous
centuries. This movement towards Christian unity has become
known as the ecumenical movement, ecumenical being derived
from a word in the Greek New Testament, *oikoumene*, meaning
the 'whole inhabited world'. The vision of the movement is of a
Christian Church united in mission and service to the whole
inhabited world. It grew out of the experience of the modern
missionary movement which found its mission to the world
fragmented and handicapped by denominational divisions and
rivalries. Its history in Protestantism is usually traced from a
great International Missionary Conference held in Edinburgh in
1910, leading to the development of various conferences and
agencies out of which grew the World Council of Churches, constituted in 1948 to enable member churches 'to meet each other,
to discuss common problems and, where possible, to formulate
common policies and take corporate action.' Geneva was chosen
as the headquarters of the Central Committee and its secretariat
presides over such important and active agencies as Christian
Aid. The W.C.C., as it is called, has always emphasised that it is
not a church but,

> a fellowship of churches which confess the Lord Jesus Christ
> as God and Saviour according to the Scriptures and therefore
> seek to fulfil together their common calling to the glory of the
> One God, Father, Son and Holy Spirit.

Irish Presbyterians were involved in the ecumenical move-

ment from its beginnings in 1910 but, in recent years, the participation of 'unreformed' churches such as the Orthodox churches
and the increasing involvement of Roman Catholics as observers
and in joint working parties led some Irish Presbyterians to
questions their church's membership of the W.C.C. The historical
experience of Irish Presbyterians has made them suspicious, on
the one hand, of Roman Catholicism, which they believe to have
made unbiblical additions to the Christian tradition, and, on the
other, of Liberal Protestants, whom they believe to have reduced
the Christian tradition to vanishing point and which, in the form
of 'political' or 'liberation' theology they perceive to be influential in the ecumenical movement. At first the movement to withdraw from the W.C.C. was resisted successfully by a majority in
the General Assembly but in the 1970s concern mounted over
the policy of the W.C.C.'s Programme to Combat Racism to give
grants to liberation movements in Africa which were known to
use violence. One such movement was the Rhodesian Patriotic
Front, campaigning to overthrow the racist regime of Ian Smith
in Rhodesia and which, it was alleged, had murdered
Pentecostal missionaries who included missionaries from
Northern Ireland. Some saw parallels with the IRA, who
claimed to be a liberation army, and in 1978 a special meeting of
the General Assembly, convened to consider the Presbyterian
Church's relations with the W.C.C., decided to suspend membership though it also set up a special committee to study what
actions the church could take against racism. The decision of the
Special Assembly was confirmed by the regular meeting of the
General Assembly in 1979, and in 1980 this became a decision to
withdraw altogether, by 448 votes to 388.

The process of withdrawal from ecumenical or inter-church
associations has continued. In 1989 the General Assembly decided
to hold aloof from a new Council of Churches of Britain and
Ireland which was replacing the British Council of Churches, of
which the Irish Presbyterian Church had been a member since
its formation in 1942. The new body was pledged to increasingly
active ecumenism 'as a dimension of all we do' and this, and the

decision of the Roman Catholic Church in Britain to participate in the new Council, undoubtedly affected the attitude of many Irish Presbyterians towards membership.

Membership has been continued of the Irish Council of Churches, the Conference of European Churches and the World Alliance of Reformed Churches. The Irish Council of Churches grew out of a number of initiatives to advance the cause of Christian unity among the Protestant churches in Ireland, beginning with a joint committee of Methodists and Presbyterians in 1922. The Church of Ireland became involved in inter-church dialogue leading to the formation of a United Council of Churches and Religious Communions in Ireland which became the Irish Council of Churches in 1966.

Through the Irish Council of Churches the Irish Presbyterian Church is involved in the Irish inter-church meeting which includes the Roman Catholic Church. The original response of the Roman Catholic Church to the Protestant ecumenical movement had been negative. To become involved would give countenance to a false Christianity quite alien to the teachings and practice of the one true church which already existed in the Roman Catholic Church. Change came, however, with the Second Vatican Council and its decree on ecumenism which made new relationships possible between Roman Catholics and those now regarded as 'separated brethren'. In 1970 a joint working party on social problems was set up by the Irish Council of Churches and the Roman Catholic hierarchy which produced a series of reports on such subjects as drug abuse, the welfare of the people and biblical teaching on peace, justice and reconciliation. This was followed in 1973 by what became known as the Ballymascanlon Talks in which contentious theological questions like the authority of the church and the problem of inter-church marriages were discussed. One working party under the joint chairmanship of Bishop Cahal Daly (later Cardinal Daly) and Methodist Eric Gallagher published a report on violence in Ireland. A later publication, *Ballymascanlon: An Irish Venture in Inter-Church Dialogue* presented summaries of papers on

Church, Scripture, Authority, Baptism, Eucharist, Marriage, Social and Community Problems, and Christianity and Secularism. In 1978 the General Assembly

> encouraged ministers, elders and church members, as part of our witness to the Reformed faith, to be more outgoing in their associations with the clergy and members of the Roman Catholic Church and encourage them where possible to study the scriptures together.

Although, in 1988, the General Assembly, after a poorly attended debate, decided to withdraw from talks which had been going on since the 1980s with the Methodist and Church of Ireland churches, about their common search for unity, on the grounds that they were going nowhere, participation in the Irish Inter-Church Meeting has continued. In the 1980s the Meeting formed an Irish Inter-Church Committee with two departments, one concerned with social, the other with theological, issues. The former has produced reports on such subjects as Marriage and the Family, Young People and the church, and Sectarianism, while the latter has produced Bible study notes and information on cults, and their reports have included Salvation and Grace, and Freedom, Justice and Responsibility in Ireland today. A re-organisation of the Inter-Church Meeting and Committee is currently going forward. Irish Presbyterians continue to encourage dialogue with Roman Catholics and co-operation in Bible study and on matters where no compromise of doctrinal clarity arises, such as questions of social justice, humanitarian issues and questions of public morality. There has been opposition to joint acts of worship and it has been emphasised that there can be no question of seeking unity with the Roman Catholic Church so long as that church holds to beliefs and practices which Presbyterians continue to consider to be unbiblical and erroneous.

In the Second Vatican Council the Roman Catholic Church sought and, to some extent, found *aggiornamento*, bringing the church up to date. Two important anniversaries – the 150th anniversary of the formation of the General Assembly in 1990 and the 350th anniversary of the formation of the first presbytery on Irish soil in 1642 – provided occasions for Irish Presbyterian self-examination. A committee set up by the General Assembly in 1988 to prepare for the two anniversaries defined their objective as 'the spiritual renewal of the church':

> The overall aim would be to celebrate our history both by humble thanksgiving for our heritage and by looking for a revitalisation of the church today as the Holy Spirit gives us a new vision of God and of the tasks he lays upon us.

A special residential meeting of the General Assembly was held in the University of Ulster in Coleraine in September 1990 with the theme 'Transformed ... Not Conformed', derived from Romans 12:2:

> Do not conform any longer to the pattern of this world, but be transformed by the renewal of your mind. Then you will be able to test and approve what God's will is – his good, pleasing and perfect will.

Looking back on the Coleraine Assembly, the committee expressed its conviction that 'their vision had been wonderfully fulfilled as the Spirit of God blew away our cobwebs and poured in his own creative power.' An important product of the Assembly was the 'Coleraine Declaration', expressing the church's penitence for failure to listen to God and to one another. Among other sins confessed were being bound to the tradition of the past, failing to challenge sectarianism and being afraid to take risks for our faith. The Declaration offered a vision of the church open and willing to listen to God's word, present in the world as Christ's love, Christ's justice and Christ's hope, affirming oneness with all who sincerely love the Lord Jesus. The Declaration acknowledged that, in Northern Ireland,

> we need great courage to work for change, and the flexibility to find new ways of enabling the two traditions to relate to one another in a positive and constructive way, developing new structures that will build trust, and help to create a first and sustainable community life for the years ahead.

Having expressed penitence for having been too much conformed to this world, in too many ways, the Declaration prayed:

God make us a joyful and expectant Church
confident in Him who has made us His people
and given us a heavenly destiny.

God make us no longer a Church of yesterday
But a Church of today and tomorrow.

God make us mindful of God's living presence
in our midst, leading us where He wants us to go,
no longer conformed to this world, its mind-set
and lifestyle but transformed by the Spirit's
renewing power.

To God be glory in the Church, now and ever.

Another residential Assembly was held, also in Coleraine, in 1997, with the title, 2020 Vision, which signified both perfect sight and an early date in the new millennium, and designed to give Irish Presbyterians a clear vision for the future. It was another stage in Irish Presbyterianism's process of *aggiornamento* and those who attended were challenged, uplifted and inspired. In particular they were challenged by the Rev Michael Cassidy from South Africa, who spoke movingly of the contribution of the churches and of prayer to the ending of *apartheid*, the transformation of a situation of hopelessness and despair into one of hope and promise. More than a thousand stood in response to his call to pledge themselves to new action for peace and reconciliation in Northern Ireland, in whatever way the Lord would lead.

The 1992 General Assembly, celebrating 350 years of Irish Presbyterian history, received and commended a Mission Statement, aimed not so much at telling the outside world what Irish Presbyterianism is about, as telling Irish Presbyterians what their calling is. Nevertheless, as a statement of how the Presbyterian Church in Ireland understands itself and its calling in today's world, as we enter the new millennium, it provides a fitting conclusion to this account of Irish Presbyterian history:

The Presbyterian Church in Ireland,
as a Reformed Church within the wider body of Christ
is grounded in the Scriptures
and exists to love and honour God
through faith in His Son and by the power of His Spirit,
and to enable her members to play their part
in fulfilling God's mission to our world.
God calls us to a shared life
in which we love, honour and are reconciled to one another
whilst respecting our diversity
within the Presbyterian Church in Ireland.
We are called to encourage
the exercise of the gifts of every member of the Body
for the work of ministry and,
seeking the renewal of the whole church
to co-operate with other parts of Christ's Church
without betrayal of our convictions.

God calls us to worship him with our whole lives,
meeting together in groups large and small
and gathering especially on the Lord's Day
for the preaching and study of His Word,
the celebration of the sacraments
and the offering of prayer and praise with reverence and joy
using language, form and music appropriate
both to Scripture and to our time and culture.
God calls us to mission as witnesses to Christ
through both evangelism and social witness
challenging the values of the world in which we live
with the values of God's kingdom
and winning men and women to faith and discipleship.
This mission is to be pursued amongst all the people of
Ireland
and the peoples of the European Community and the whole
world:
those with whom we feel comfortable,

those from whom we feel alienated
and those who are in any way distant from us
in culture and faith.

We ourselves are challenged with a biblical discipleship
which is radical
in its self-denial
simplicity of lifestyle
stewardship of money
faithful relationships
prayerfulness,
concern for the world which God has created
and love for its people whom He loves
and for who salvation He gave His Son.

Select Bibliography
Books and articles cited, in order of citation

R. Blair, *Autobiography and Life*, ed. T. McCrie (Edinburgh 1848).

P. Adair, *A True Narrative of the Rise and Progress of the Presbyterian Church in Ireland, 1623-70*, ed. W.D. Killen (Belfast 1886).

J. Livingstone, *Life*, ed. W.K. Tweedie (1847).

A. Ford, J. McGuire and K. Milne, (eds.), *By Law Established: The Church of Ireland Since the Reformation* (1995).

M. Perceval-Maxwell, *The Scottish Migration to Ulster in the Reign of James I* (1973).

K. Herlihy, (ed.), *The Religion of Irish Dissent* (1996).

W. D. Bailie, *The Six Mile Water Revival of 1625* (1996).

M. Westerkamp, *The Triumph of the Laity: Scots-Irish Piety and the Great Awakening* (1988).

J. Seaton Reid, *History of the Presbyterian Church in Ireland,* 3 Vols (1867).

W. T. Latimer, *History of the Irish Presbyterians* (1902)

D. Miller, *Queen's Rebels. Ulster Loyalism in Historical Perspective* (1978).

St. J. D. Seymour, *The Puritans in Ireland 1647-1661* (1921).

G. R. Cragg, *From Puritanism to the Age of Reason* (1950).

Ian McBride, *Scripture Politics. Ulster Presbyterianism and Irish Radicalism in the Late Eighteenth Century* (1998).

Ian Hazlett, *Traditions of Theology in Glasgow, 1450-1990* (1993).

L. E. Schmidt, *Holy Fairs: Scottish Communions and American Revivals in the Early Modern Period* (1989).

Henry Montgomery, 'Outlines of the History of Presbyterianism in Ireland', *Bible Christian* 2 (1847).

S. E. Ahlstrom, *A Religious History of the American People* (1972).

A. T. Q. Stewart, *The Narrow Ground* (1997).

W. Campbell, 'Sketches of the History of the Presbyterians In Ireland', 1803 ms. Presbyterian Historical Society, Belfast.

A. T. Q. Stewart, 'A Stable Unseen Power. Dr William Drennan and the Origins of the United Irishmen'. J. Boss and P. Jupp, *Essays Presented to Michael Roberts* (1976).

D. A. Chart (ed.), *The Drennan Letters* (1931).

D. Miller, 'Presbyterians and "Modernization" in Ulster', *Past and Present* 80 (1978).

R. Musgrave, *Memoirs of the Different Rebellions in Ireland* (1802).

J. Oman, *The Problem of Faith and Freedom* (1906).

J. M. Barkley, *A Short History of the Presbyterian Church in Ireland* (1959).

W. R. Ward, 'The Evangelical Revival', S. Gilley and W.J. Sheils (eds.), *A History of Religion in Britain* (1994).

J. E. Davey, *The Story of a Hundred Years* (1940).

J. Jamieson, *History of the Royal Belfast Academical Institution* (1959).

D. Bowen, *The Protestant Crusade in Ireland* (1978).

R. J. Rodgers, 'Vision Unrealized: The Presbyterian Mission to Irish Roman Catholics in the Nineteenth Century', *The Bulletin of the Irish Presbyterian Historical Society of Ireland*, Vol. 20, March 1991.

D. Bowen, *Paul, Cardinal Cullen and the Shaping of Modern Irish Catholicism* (1983).

R. J. Rodgers, 'Presbyterian "Alternative Schools" in the Nineteenth Century', R.F.G. Holmes and D.B. Knox (eds.) *The General Assembly of the Irish Presbyterian Church in Ireland 1840-1990* (1990).

H. Magee, *Fifty Years in the Irish Mission*, nd.

J. Bardon, *History of Ulster* (1992).

A. R. Scott, *The Ulster Revival of 1859* (1994).

D. Hempton and M. Hill, *Evangelical Protestantism in Ulster Society 1740-1890* (1992).

R. Coad, *A History of the Brethren Movement* (1974).

P. Miller, *The Life of the Mind in America from the Revolution to the Civil War* (1965).

J. Kent, *Holding the Fort: Studies in Victorian Revivalism* (1978).

G. Marsden, *The Evangelical Mind and the New School Presbyterian Experience* (1970).

M. Noll, *The Scandal of the Evangelical Mind* (1994).

R. Allen, *The Presbyterian College. A Centenary History* (1953).

R. F. G. Holmes, *Magee College 1865-1965* (1965).

J. J. Shaw, *Mr Gladstone's Two Irish Policies, 1869 and 1886* (1888).

P. J. Buckland, *A Factory of Grievances* (1979).

R. S. Tosh, 'One Hundred and Fifty Years of Worship. A Survey' in Holmes and Knox, as above.

J. Thompson (ed.), *Into All The World. A History of the Overseas Work of the Presbyterian Church in Ireland, 1840-1990* (1990).

J. A. Mackay, *Christianity on the Frontier* (1950).

D. Bebbington, *The Non-Conformist Conscience* (1982).

D. Kennedy, *The Widening Gulf. Northern Ireland Attitudes to the Independent Irish State, 1919-48* (1988).

M. Harris, *The Catholic Church and the Establishment of Northern Ireland* (1992).

A. A. Fulton, *Biography of Ernest Davey* (1970).

D. Cooke, *Persecuting Zeal. A Portrait of Ian Paisley* (1996).

Index

Principal names and subjects